Baptism Matters

Baptism Matters

NICK AND HAZEL WHITEHEAD

The National Society
A Christian Voice in Education

a co-publication with
Church House Publishing

National Society/Church House Publishing
Church House
Great Smith Street
London
SW1P 3NZ

First published in 1998 by The National Society/Church House Publishing

ISBN 0 7151 4900 8

Photocopying

Cover design by Julian Smith

Printed by The Cromwell Press Ltd, Trowbridge, Wiltshire

CONTENTS

ACKNOWLEDGEMENTS

The publisher gratefully acknowledges permission to reproduce copyright material in this book. Every effort has been made to trace and contact copyright holders. If there are any inadvertent omissions we apologise to those concerned and will ensure that a suitable acknowledgement is made at the next reprint.

Extracts from *The Canons of the Church of England*, Church House Publishing, 5th edition, 1993 and *Common Worship: Initiation Services*, Church House Publishing, 1998 are copyright © The Central Board of Finance of the Church of England and are reproduced by permission.

Prayer (pp. 65-6) from Christopher Herbert (compiler), *Prayers for Children*, National Society/Church House Publishing, 1993 is copyright © Christopher Herbert and is reproduced by permission.

The Scripture quotations contained herein are from the New Revised Standard Version Bible, copyright © 1989 by the Division of Christian Education of the National Council of the Churches of Christ in the USA and are used by permission. All rights reserved.

INTRODUCTION

'I went to the church to find you and you wasn't there. It's impor-tant.We've had a baby and we want him done. Can I bring him round this afternoon?'

'I don't know whether you can help. I'd really like to talk about a christening but I'm divorced. Will you still christen my baby?'

'How much will a baptism cost and can I pay in instalments?'

To regular churchgoers and committed Christians these questions may seem far-fetched, naive or unreal. They demonstrate (because they *are* genuine quotes from parents) a deep-seated need to engage with the church and/or with God and a strong desire to bring children for baptism. Baptism may be subject to popular misconceptions and misunderstood, but it is as live an issue now as it has ever been.

The new generation of liturgies, *Common Worship*, has arisen after many years of work, debate and discussion and is the product of serious thinking and experimentation. The initiation rites provide fresh opportunities for all those engaged in delivering practical ministry within parochial contexts to reconsider the meaning of baptismal liturgy and their own approach to it. It means, too, that ministers (both ordained and lay) must find ways of engaging the minds and hearts of their congregations with the style and content of the new texts and together relate it to the communities among whom they live and work.

The Church of England has not been alone in its desire to revise and revisit worship; there have been parallel movements within the Roman Catholic and Methodist Churches and this new era should be embraced by Christians of every denomination as a time when, once again, new life is being breathed into the worship which is at the centre of their Christian lives.

The revised initiation rites, published as *Common Worship: Initiation Services*, are the first to be available to the Anglican Communion and were authorized for use from Easter Eve 1998. They provide a variety of services including Baptism at a Service of the Word, Baptism with Holy Communion, with Confirmation, and in an emergency, as well as rites for the reception of others into the Anglican Communion and adult reaffirmation of baptismal vows.

Baptism Matters aims to consider the content and practicalities of the new liturgy, but within the context of the past. It is a book based on reason and experience, with a nod in the direction of Scripture and tradition, and provides food for reflection for those involved in the day-to-day ministry of the Church, whether as lay or ordained. It will be particularly helpful for Readers, those training for, or new to, full-time ministry, baptism visitors and all those coming to terms with the implementation of the new liturgy. It is hoped that the mood of the book will encourage many members of local congregations to partic-ipate in the discussion and work surrounding baptism matters, from the first phone call through to confirmation.

More academic works will provide for those who wish to grapple with theological minutiae, but the first two chapters of this book discuss some of the scriptural evidence and outline some typical baptism poli-cies in operation within the Church of England. Chapter 3 places the issue of baptism within the context of the Church's life and shows it as one part of the whole jigsaw of ministry.

The next chapter considers the nature and purpose of preparing people for baptism, whatever role they play in the procedure, and gives brief outlines of the different levels of preparation offered or required by particular churches. Chapter 5 examines the role of god-parents in an attempt to give them a higher profile in general and suggests specific ways of including them in the life of the child they have agreed to support.

Chapter 6 goes to the heart of the matter, discussing the new rites in some detail and highlighting especially the new emphases and the various options for worship. If you are primarily interested in the new baptism rites, then you might want to begin by reading this chapter. Chapter 7 deals with the more practical aspects of the service, with many ideas and resources for appropriate talks to use at all-age worship and other ways of involving children and adults in worship.

On the basis that baptism is one part of the journey for those 'on the way', the final chapter investigates the best ways to follow up families and keep them journeying alongside the local church community.

This book draws on wide experience of ministry in the parish and will complement other material produced in the light of the welcome advent of *Common Worship*.

SECTION ONE

Baptism:
The Foundations
of Ministry

1

THE SACRAMENT
OF BAPTISM

The Anglican Communion continues to believe that baptism is very important both to individuals and to the wider Church. It is the fundamental act of Christian initiation, attested in Scripture, well documented throughout the tradition of the Church and widely practised. It is the sacrament which unites Christians to Christ and makes them part of his body, the worldwide Church.

What is a sacrament?

Christians agree in understanding baptism to be one of the two major sacraments, the other being the Eucharist. What is more contentious is the interpretation of the nature of sacraments and who should be allowed to receive them. Our answers to these questions will affect our relations with other Christians who start from a different understanding and will influence the way we formulate baptismal policy.

Throughout the tradition of the Church, sacraments have been described in a variety of ways, some more lucid than others. The kind of language used, however, implies much common ground.

Tertullian (160–225) is said to have been the first to introduce into Christian thinking the word '*sacramentum*', which was the Latin translation of the Greek word '*mysterion*'; but it was Augustine (354–430) who really developed the discussion. He defined a sacrament as 'the visible form of invisible grace' or 'a sign of a sacred thing'. His principles were that

> *A sacrament is a sign. Signs, when applied to divine things, are called sacraments. The sign must bear some relation to the thing*

> which is signified. *If sacraments do not bear some resemblance to
> the things of which they are the sacraments, they would not be
> sacraments at all.*[1]

Augustine also made clear that although the Church had the right and
duty to authorize ministers to administer sacraments, their efficacy
did not depend upon the personal qualities of the minister but only on
the grace of Christ. This is very helpful for those who administer the
sacraments, because it assures them that their own inadequacy and
sinfulness do not diminish the effect of a sacrament. It also underlines
that the sacraments are gifts which come from the grace of Christ
alone and do not depend on what the recipient deserves. Augustine's
doctrine of prevenient grace suggests that God's grace is active in
human lives long before the individual realizes it and it works silently
towards a personal conversion or turning to Christ.

Augustine takes this even further in his doctrine of operative grace,
which stresses that conversion relies solely on the work of God and is
effected by him rather than by anything the recipient may say or do. It
is only after conversion that individuals have a part to play because
they are then ready, willing and able to work with God in the process
of salvation and liberation. This is called co-operative grace. This
understanding of how God's grace can work has a profound effect on
baptismal policy. Some will want to defer the act of baptism until such
time as co-operative grace has come into play and the recipient (or at
least the parents) are fully converted.

Others will happily see it as belonging to the time of God's operative
grace and therefore allow baptism to occur even when the received
faith and response of the individual is not clearly defined.

The debate rests on whether baptism, a sign of belonging and salvation, is
a reward for good works, good behaviour or sufficient faith, or a free offer
of grace dependent entirely upon the goodness and generosity of God.

The traditional Anglican position as stated in *The Book of Common Prayer*
is that a sacrament is 'an outward and visible sign of an inward and
spiritual grace given unto us, ordained by Christ himself as a means
whereby we receive the same and a pledge to assure us thereof'.[2] It is
this statement which continues to define the Church of England's
understanding of baptism.

The theological significance of sacraments implicit here involves three major principles. The first is that sacraments are incarnational, they make clear the unbreakable link between the divine and the human (perfectly expressed in Jesus Christ) and use an actual or material form to embody a spiritual reality. Secondly, the divine action upon the human person is objective and does not depend on the changing or subjective response of the recipient but on obedience to the divine will. This means that however unworthy, inadequate or sinful the recipient (and we would argue that we are never anything but sinful), the sacrament exists and is effective in its own right. The recipient can, however, limit this effectiveness by putting an 'impediment' in the way of grace so that the sacrament is not as effective as it might be if the individual was co-operating with God. Thirdly, sacraments are more than a private and personal relationship between God and the individual; they are part of the social structure because they are mediated through the Church. Thus, a priest cannot celebrate the Eucharist on his or her own without the people and hence the importance of public baptism.

The three 'rights'

For a sacrament to be valid it must fulfil minimal conditions which have long been considered necessary: the right matter (water in the case of baptism) and the right form (the words) must be used with the right intention. These conditions ensure that the sacrament is proper and will convey the grace of God regardless of the moral, spiritual or physical state of the recipient. In baptism, it is very clear whether the right matter and words have been used; it is less easy to define the right intention. Is it the individual, the priest or the Church who must have the right intention? And how can such an intention be defined or measured?

What are sacraments for?

Alister McGrath[3] describes four key purposes of sacraments: they convey grace (as well as being signs of it); they strengthen faith (which must be weak because it is human); they enhance unity and commitment within the Church through common sacramental experience; and they reassure us of God's promises towards us.

This echoes what Article XXV says:

> *Sacraments ordained of Christ be not only badges or tokens of Christian men's profession, but rather they be certain sure witnesses, and effectual signs of grace, and God's good will towards us, by the which he doth work invisibly in us, and doth not only quicken, but also strengthen and confirm our Faith in him.*

It is interesting to note that there is nothing in Article XXV which requires anything of the recipient. The initiative comes from God and the work is his. Seen in this light, baptism is a conveyor of grace, a sign of God's good will towards us, a means of bringing to life and strengthening faith, a way for God to work in us invisibly and a vehicle for enhancing commitment. This will feed our discussion on how the practice of baptism is approached in our parishes.

How many sacraments are there?

The Councils of Florence (1439) and Trent (1546) ratified the existence of seven sacraments: baptism, confirmation, the Eucharist, penance, extreme unction, ordination and matrimony. They said that Christ instituted all these in the Scriptures; where scriptural evidence was tenuous, they provided some scant evidence to show that he could, with a stretch of the imagination, be seen as their source.

This was challenged during the Reformation by Luther, who sought to rectify the Catholic position. His conclusion was that there were only two true sacraments, 'baptism and bread', because only here could the Word of God and an outward sacramental sign (water, bread and wine) be found.

Since then, the tradition of the Church has recognized only two genuine sacraments: 'There are two Sacraments ordained of Christ our Lord in the Gospel, that is to say, Baptism, and the Supper of the Lord.' Yet it has continued to give some importance to the lesser sacraments, while acknowledging

> *that the five commonly called Sacraments, that is to say, Confirmation, Penance, Orders, Matrimony, and Extreme Unction, are not to be counted for Sacraments of the Gospel, being such as have grown partly of the corrupt following of the Apostles, partly are states of life allowed in the Scriptures.*[4]

The sacrament of baptism

For the purposes of this book, it is enough to know that baptism has been accorded a high place as a major sacrament in the thinking and activity of the Church. We can see how the detail has changed in the course of history, with changing cultures and contexts and as a result of reason and experience. For example:

- In the fifth and sixth centuries, when the infant mortality rate was particularly high and it was believed that the unbaptized went to hell, babies were baptized as a matter of course. Few believe this now in their rational moments, but the legacy still lingers deep down in the subconscious.

- When adult baptism by full immersion entailed removing all clothing, baptism was conducted in private to preserve modesty and this may be why many still fight shy of public display.

- The exorcism (which was abolished in the 1552 Prayer Book revision) was necessary in an age which held strong beliefs about witchcraft and the activity of the devil, but may be completely inappropriate as we approach the millennium.

Articles in theological dictionaries on the development of baptismal practices make interesting reading.

Liturgy and the theology of baptism

In Chapter 6 we shall examine the new rites in some detail and highlight the changes which have arisen. The new liturgy is founded on the rich inheritance of *The Book of Common Prayer* and *The Alternative Service Book* and it is helpful to bear this in mind when approaching the new rites.

The BCP preserves Catholic teaching and in the first prayers in the baptismal liturgy maintains quite clearly the doctrine of baptismal regeneration which says that human beings are washed and sanctified by the Holy Ghost, delivered from the wrath of God, received into the ark of Christ's Church and granted remission of sins. The sinful state of humanity and fear of hell and the wrath of God are well documented in the liturgy, implicitly and explicitly. It assumes that the sacrament is valid regardless of the condition of the recipient but puts the onus on the child to fulfil his or her part of the bargain in these

7

words, which appear in the priest's address to the 'godfathers and god-mothers':

> *this Infant must also faithfully, for his part, promise by you that*
> *are his sureties, (until he comes of age to take it upon himself,)*
> *that he will renounce the devil and all his works, and constantly*
> *believe God's holy Word, and obediently keep his commandments.*

The sign is there but requires a response for its true effect to be realized.

The ASB follows broadly similar lines to the BCP, although it provides for baptism to take place during the Eucharist and there are changes in the statements made by parents and godparents. No longer do we find them renouncing the 'devil and all his works, the vain pomp and glory of the world, with all covetous desires of the same, and the carnal desires of the flesh'; now they simply renounce 'evil'.

Of course, in the seventeenth century, it was far easier to discern who was a member of the Church of England, at least in name, and so there was no need for a debate about the uncommitted and fringe members of the congregation such as we have today.

However, the traditions and liturgy of the Church did not develop in a vacuum; they were based on an acceptance of the prime importance of Scripture and it is to this that we now turn.

In the Scriptures

THE OLD TESTAMENT

Old Testament theology is based on the idea of the covenant between God and human beings and much of the material deals with this relationship. There are covenants with Abraham,[5] based on God's promises and his election of Israel and recognized by circumcision, which marks out the people of God from the nations; and also the covenant with Moses,[6] based on the promise of the land, the giving of the Law and the demand for obedience from the people.

The children of Abraham received the sign of circumcision almost from birth because they were part of the people of Israel by virtue of their nationality. This did not guarantee that they would be loyal and faithful men of God (and it said nothing, of course, about the women) and it is very easy to find stories of those who clearly did not become such paragons of holiness. Even kings, priests and leaders failed to live up to the demands of the covenant.

The covenant relationship underlying the Old Testament narrative depends primarily on the sovereignty of God, hence the many occurrences of the phrase 'I am the Lord your God'. It was his choice, his love and his faithfulness which were the givens in the unequal equation (unequal because God is God and human beings are not). For the relationship to be fulfilled, an obedient, humble and loyal response from the people was the ideal but not the norm. It is with the knowledge of this inheritance that we approach our Christian faith.

THE BAPTISM OF JESUS

The fact that Jesus himself was baptized is used as a marker that this is something to be taken seriously. There is well-attested evidence in the synoptic gospels that Jesus was baptized in the River Jordan by John the Baptist[7] and an allusion to the baptism tradition in John's gospel,[8] but it comes as no surprise to find that these four accounts, presumably of the same event, are not identical. While the differences are interesting for biblical scholars, they do not contribute much to the modern debate about baptism policy.

In Mark's account, people from 'the whole Judean countryside and all the people of Jerusalem' (1.5) are baptized before Jesus, the implication being that Jesus is unique and yet 'one of the crowd', sharing in a common experience with local villagers. In typical Marcan style, the account is short and to the point. The Spirit is seen descending like a dove and the voice from heaven is heard – but by Jesus alone.

Matthew's account has small variations. It implies that Jesus' journey to the Jordan was more purposeful: 'Then Jesus came . . . to be baptized' (3.13) and that the Baptist, who had recognized Jesus' importance, was reluctant to oblige. The purpose of the baptism is said to be 'to fulfil all righteousness'.

Luke's account, despite a long preamble, is understated, giving no purpose, conversation or detail other than the descent of the dove and the voice from heaven, but it is assumed that John's baptism is one of 'repentance for the forgiveness of sins' (3.3).

What all three have in common is a connection between baptism, repentance and confession, plus the declaration that although John himself baptizes with water, the one who comes will baptize with the Spirit.

Jesus' baptism might encourage us to think that baptism is a 'good thing', but it cannot be seen as a blueprint for modern initiation rites. Repentance, a statement of faith, belonging to the community, dying with Christ: all these are part of our understanding of baptism but can they be applied to Jesus? The account of his baptism provides a back-cloth for spelling out exactly who Jesus is. The descent of the dove and the voice from heaven are reminders of the divine presence, divine approval and the possibility of some new divine activity. This is a pivotal moment for the ministry which is to begin with a vengeance, a turning towards the new mission and a commitment to all it entailed, including suffering and death.

BAPTISM IN THE GOSPELS

Mark makes scant reference to baptism but where he does it appears to be something which makes serious demands. To James and John, who want to sit on his right and left hand, Jesus uses baptism in the context of dying and suffering. The word used here is 'reminiscent in contemporary Greek of being flooded with calamities'[9] and the disciples' easy acceptance of this kind of baptism demonstrates their lack of understanding of the consequences of aligning themselves with Jesus in this way.

At the end of the gospel, Mark's Jesus is quite unequivocal in what he says to the eleven: 'Go into all the world and proclaim the good news to the whole creation. The one who believes and is baptized will be saved; but the one who does not believe will be condemned.'[10]

For Mark, we note that:

- the mission is universal;

- the importance of belief is stressed;

- baptism is a response to the gospel message;

- we do not know what happens to those who believe but are not baptized, nor to those who are baptized but subsequently lose faith;

10

- there are no other examples of baptisms taking place.

In the Great Commission in Matthew's gospel,[11] we find Jesus issuing a final command to the eleven to 'Go, therefore, and make disciples of all nations, baptizing them in the name of the Father and of the Son and of the Holy Spirit and teaching them to obey everything that I have commanded you.' Scholars may contest the authenticity of what they see as a late addendum to Matthew's gospel, but whether these are the original words of Jesus or attributable to others, they highlight some interesting features:

- the mission is now universal and to 'all nations';

- the exact meaning of 'making disciples' is unclear;

- there is no direct reference to faith, repentance or joining the Church, although these may be implicitly assumed;

- it is not clear whether the acts of making disciples, baptizing and teaching are meant to occur concurrently or consecutively;

- this is the first reference to threefold baptism since the first disciples baptized 'in the name of Jesus' only.

Luke sheds no light on the matter; in his account of Jesus commissioning his disciples there is no reference to baptism at all, even though 'repentance and forgiveness of sins is to be proclaimed in his name to all nations'.[12]

John's gospel has Jesus baptizing people in Judea while John baptized others at Aenon near Salim because people 'kept coming'.[13] There are no other details except to note that these verses are part of a chapter dealing with light and darkness, salvation and condemnation. We are not told whether John assumes that baptism implies belief.

BAPTISM IN THE EARLY CHURCH

In the book of Acts, where we see the early Christians at work, the number of baptisms recorded suggests that it was a regular feature of the Church's work. Pentecost[14] is the first explicit example of the baptism of believers. Repentance had to precede baptism, which was in the name of Christ for the forgiveness of sins and would lead to the gift of the Holy Spirit. We are told that 'those who welcomed his [Peter's] message were baptized', about three thousand in number, and that afterwards they devoted themselves to teaching, fellowship, the breaking of bread and prayer. We have no knowledge of the long-term effects, the content of the preparation or the criteria used for judging the quality of individual faith.

Paul himself is an ideal adult baptism candidate for those who like to have a biblical model, and a prime example of a convert who changed his lifestyle completely, repented of his past and went on to work tirelessly for his Lord and Saviour. In the account in Acts 9.17-19 he is baptized after his blinding vision and the regaining of his sight.

Not all cases are as dramatic and there is no blueprint. Many features appear but there are contradictions and variants. We need to note these factors:

- Baptism often occurs almost immediately after the preaching of the word (or at least that is the way the writer presents it). It is administered on demand and at the nearest appropriate place after hearing a sermon or having a conversation with no chance of weighing up the lasting nature of the convert's faith. The jailer[15] and the eunuch[16] both fall into this category. This is a far cry from the thorough preparation of later centuries, involving fasting, exorcism, lengthy confessions and a long catechumenate.

- Baptism often follows the explicit profession of belief and/or repentance, as in the case of Simon the magician and other Samaritans,[17] or implied faith as in the case of Lydia and her household,[18] where all we are told is that the Lord 'opened her heart'.

- Gentiles were able to receive baptism.[19]

- The Holy Spirit sometimes came before baptism[20] and sometimes after.[21]

- Baptism could be administered in private,[22] in the household[23] or with a cast of thousands.[24]

BAPTISM IN PAUL

Baptism had become the normal procedure when Paul made his appearance and he was baptized himself after his conversion experience.[25] It is assumed that Christians will be baptized[26] because this is the norm, and Paul's understanding of what that means is found in many places throughout his writings.

For Paul, baptism means:

- being washed clean and forgiven or put right with God;
- being made holy;[27]
- belonging to the community of faith with responsibilities to other members of the community;
- being part of the body of Christ in the world;
- receiving the gift of the Holy Spirit;[28]
- embracing the death of Christ and being buried with him;
- as a result of this death and burial, sharing in the resurrection of Christ;[29]
- walking in newness of life;[30]
- working for unity;[31]
- being clothed/putting on Christ.[32]

But many of these features can be found elsewhere in Paul as part of his whole theology, with no reference to baptism *per se*. Paul seems to assume that those who are baptized have faith, and vice versa, but it is noteworthy that in his letters he admonishes and encourages local congregations who are not living up to their baptismal promises. His concerns are not so much with who should be baptized but with the behaviour and attitudes of those who are full members of the churches. Once again, we find few paragons of holiness.

What is evident from our brief summary of the foundations from Scripture and tradition is that, as usual, there is no simple, uncontentious directive which we can apply to our ministry as we reach the year 2000. Biblical evidence must be taken in context and examined in far greater detail than there is space to do here; the tradition is a moving and living thing which responds to new ways of thinking and believing. Scripture and tradition underpin our faith, but where there is ambiguity they must be used as tools in the current debate rather than enslaving us. It is possible, as we have seen and shall see again in

Chapter 2, to find evidence for almost any baptismal policy. This uncertainty should be seen as both challenge and opportunity by those who have to share decision-making about practical ministry.

❷

ANGLICAN
BAPTISMAL POLICY

Within the spectrum of the Anglican Communion, there are extremes of belief and policy in the matter of baptism. These variations in practice are based on sincerely-held views about the nature of baptism which should be listened to with care. It is easier to respect those whose policies are at variance with our own when we understand what is behind their thinking and the different interpretations of Scripture and theology on which they are based.

Under Canon Law (Canon B22), a member of the clergy may not refuse to baptize a child living in his or her parish who is brought to him or her for baptism, provided the legal requirements regarding prior notice and in relation to the godparents (see pp. 35–6) are compiled with. The minister may only delay the baptism in order to prepare or instruct the parents, guardians or godparents, and may not delay even for that reason where the child's state of health is such as to give rise to an emergency situation.

Parents sometimes feel that the member of the clergy is in substance refusing to baptize their child, because the hurdles which are placed in the way of the baptism are ones they feel unable to surmount, or that the baptism is being delayed for an unreasonable time. In that event, the parents have a right to take the matter to the bishop; the bishop must consult the member of the clergy concerned and then give such directions as he thinks fit. So the minister cannot unduly delay or refuse baptism, though few applicants are aware of this (although at least a week's prior notice is required for a baptism); but he or she should instruct the parents that the same responsibilites rest on them as on the godparents. The way this instruction is interpreted gives rise to discrepancies in practice. At one end of the spectrum there are those who impose quite stingent conditions, which make baptism obtainable only by the most persistent. At the other end are those who indiscriminately baptize 'anything that moves', with no regard for recognized parish boundaries. There are, naturally, others whose practice lies somewhere between the two extremes. There are problems with most approaches; in this chapter we shall look at four of them in greater detail.

Baptism to avoid the jaws of hell

This view comes from the Catholic tradition and, although it may not be recognized or supported by any of the established churches in the late twentieth century, vestiges of the inheritance remain. Buried deep within some people is a conviction that baptism is essential to ensure acceptance into heaven. Baptism is for these people a protection or immunization against eternal damnation. The sacrament is effective in itself, regardless of personal response or worthiness, provided it is administered under the Church's authority.

Arguments from tradition are used to support this view, together with the suggestion that the consequences of remaining unbaptized could be so awful that it is not worth taking the risk. The faith of the Church is more important than individual faith so whether the recipient is personally able to make a commitment is irrelevant. Against the theory is the contention that this smacks of superstition; experience of a loving creator and redeemer as manifested in the creation and incarnation makes this a wholly offensive and unacceptable theology.

Believers' baptism (by implication, for teenagers and adults only)

Proponents of this approach believe that only those who have themselves professed a convinced and convincing faith in Jesus Christ should be baptized. Faith must come before baptism and the signs of faith must be clearly visible. Baptism is the end result of, or the reward for, personal conversion.

Proponents of this view use the following kinds of argument:

- Scripture is of prime importance: only those who professed a personal faith were baptized in the New Testament; for example, 'Those who received his [Peter's] words were baptized'.[2]

16

- Infants are unable to demonstrate belief in the saving work of Christ and should not be baptized.

- There is no explicit evidence that infants were baptized in the early Church.

- Indiscriminate baptism may lead to the Christian faith becoming nothing more than a social convenience and the cheapening of God's grace.

To counter these arguments, others say that the scriptural evidence varies: some seemed to be baptized on very little evidence of faith, and whole households, presumably including children, received baptism. They speak also of baptism being a gift which cannot be earned by faith or works; it is the beginning of a journey rather than a sign of arrival. They may cite Canon Law, which speaks of baptism for all who seek it (within certain parameters), and worry about the pastoral implications of refusal.

This approach implies that the sacrament of baptism is declarative; that is, it declares what has already taken place within the individual. Baptism is a marker that the person baptized has seen the light, repented of sins and has faith in the trinitarian God. Thus it may occur when, and only when, these things are evident to the Church. If this is the premise, then clearly baptism should not be administered to any child, or indiscriminately to adults.

Infant baptism for the children of believing and committed parents

Supporters of this view are quite prepared to baptize infants provided they are sure that the parents have enough faith and understanding to bring up the child according to Christian principles. In reality, the criteria used to make judgements about the quality and permanence of the parents' faith must be largely subjective, but signposts which point to commitment would be attendance at worship and baptism classes.

Proponents of this view would say:

- Baptism is effective and makes sense only if it is clear that the child will be brought up in a Christian home, brought to church and taught the faith.

17

- The beginning of a journey of faith must be just that – a clear beginning, not a journey which ends as soon as the service is over.

- The Church is colluding in hypocrisy if there is no evidence to suggest this will be the case.

- The children of believers are part of the covenant community and should have the sign of belonging.

- Whole households were baptized in the New Testament.

- The Church may lose its holiness if non-believers are admitted.

The major problem with this view is that it assumes that baptism is a gift which is only available under certain conditions which the parents must meet. It is as though the child is being granted or denied the gift of the Spirit by virtue of the parents' commitment or lack of it; but even the faith of regular, paid-up members of the congregation can be severely lacking in maturity or depth, and others may fall by the wayside despite the best intentions. The theory relies heavily on co-operative grace at the expense of prevenient and operative grace. Churches which operate this policy will have different methods of assessing belonging and commitment, some more stringent than others.

> *At St James we take seriously the notion that baptism requires a real understanding of the Christian faith and so we will not even discuss baptism until parents have been on an Alpha Course and made a real commitment to Jesus Christ. Until then, we are happy to welcome them to Church, to provide a Thanksgiving for Birth service but baptism itself is not on the agenda for some time. We don't want it to be taken too lightly; nor do we want to put people in a position where they are hypocritical.[3]*

Open policy – infant baptism for any child presented to the Church

The open policy begins from a belief that baptism is a free gift from God, graciously and generously given to all who would receive it and that, although the faith of individuals or their parents may be limited or questionable, the faith of the Church will make up for such deficiencies. This is what one parish priest writes about his open policy:

> *St Nicolas' Parish Church is the parish church and its doors are open to all comers, no matter where they lie on the spectrum of Christian witness. Bearing in mind we are dealing with a fairly settled community and that Christian lives can be developed over a life-span of 70 years, our Christian approach is one of generosity, welcome, nurture and support . . . You cannot 'manage' people, especially in England, nor bend them unwillingly to your way. Christian nurturing must be done without any sign of rejection but continually, patiently and with a loving welcome discerning both the need and where the family is in its understanding of Christian commitment. I cannot emphasize enough that rejection is often perceived by parents even when not meant by the parish priest. It is so easy for a priest to condemn a family to Christian oblivion through insensitivity, rigidity and a lack of Christian love.*[4]

The main arguments in favour of this approach are as follows:

- Faith is difficult to measure. Any parents who bring their children for baptism have some faith and this should be honoured and used as a basis on which to build.

- Baptism is not a reward dependent upon faith (of child or parent) or works, but a gift which may be the beginning of a new journey and which should not be withheld from any who desire it.

- Canon Law means that baptism cannot be refused to anybody who lives within the parish boundaries.

- Parents have a major role in the Christian upbringing of their child but share that responsibility with the Church, whose collective faith will compensate for the inadequacy of the individual's faith.

- Much pastoral damage has been done by refusing baptism.

- The Church should meet people where they are and repentance and the increase of faith may come after baptism.

- Whole households, including infants, were baptized in the New Testament.

- Baptism is only one part in the process of faith development and belonging.

- The Church should be prepared to accept blurred edges in its membership and be inclusive rather than exclusive.

Others will counter that:

- baptism is trivialized and becomes a nonsense unless there are clear indications that the child will be brought up in a Christian home;

- the offer of God's grace may be abused and does not come cheaply;

- parents do understand why baptism is refused when the reasons are explained to them;

- they gain much from preparation courses, even if they come unwillingly at first;

- a Service of Thanksgiving is always available to those not ready for baptism.

Those who promote an open policy vary considerably in the style and quantity of preparation they provide for parents. An open policy does not mean that there is no preparation or that no challenges are put before parents; rather, it means that in the end baptism will be given to any who ask for it.

Ultimately, every congregation must take responsibility for working out its own baptismal policy, bearing in mind the legal requirements of Canon Law and the possible consequences to all involved. Whatever your policy, it should be clear that baptism is an important event in the life-cycle of faith for the family, the child, the couple or single parent and the Church. Every opportunity should be taken to make the family welcome and to treat them with care and consideration at what is a very important moment in their lives. However, this need not deter any congregation from seizing this prime opportunity and taking active steps to encourage baptism families into more active participation and deeper commitment.

In the end, perhaps we need to remind ourselves of two important things: it is the Church which serves the world rather than the other way round; and sacraments are given through God's grace, not ours.

It may be possible to agree with those statements and yet hold, with integrity, any of the above positions. Let John Macquarrie have the last word in this chapter:

> . . . *in any encounter with God, he has the initiative. He comes to us before we think of seeking him. We can never, as it were, manipulate God or have him at our disposal. . . it is not our faith or our expectation or our activity, still less is it the power of the priest, that produces the encounter with God.*[5]

How we interpret that encounter and what we do practically cannot be prescribed.

Emergency baptism

Every minister will have the unhappy experience of sharing in occasions when babies are born prematurely, with severe disabilities or with the strong possibility that they will die very quickly. Although baptism is no longer seen as prerequisite for entry into heaven, many parents will want an emergency baptism for their baby. A suitable short service is found on page 94 of *Common Worship: Initiation Services* and any minister or lay Christian can administer baptism in these circumstances. Details should be passed on to those responsible for ongoing pastoral care as soon as possible. If the baby subsequently lives, he or she cannnot be rebaptized but should be brought to church for a modified service of thanksgiving.

Deacons and baptism

Baptism is a sacrament and should be administered by a priest or Bishop when he is present. However, if a priest is not available, deacons may be instructed by their incumbents to baptize but this should be seen as the exception rather than the norm. Both priest and deacon work under episcopal authority in this as in any sphere.

❸

BAPTISM AND THE LIFE
OF THE CHURCH

Context and resources

Most clergy want to fulfil two objectives in baptism. First, they want
to respond positively and warmly to every request for baptism and
make every family feel valued by the church community (and, conse-
quently, by God). Secondly, they want the event to have integrity for
the church community (countering arguments that the sacrament is
sometimes devalued) and for the parents and godparents, so that they
are comfortable with the promises and declarations they are asked to
make. In practice, the extent to which these objectives can be fulfilled
depends on several factors:

- the theology and personality of the minister or ministry team;

- the tradition of the church;

- available resources;

- community expectations (in the light of the parish's historical
  response to baptism requests);

- numbers (which can vary from single figures to over 70 or 80
  per annum).

For the clergy, baptism can be both an opportunity and a threat. Each
time they respond positively to a request for baptism they hope that it
will lead to a greater commitment to Jesus Christ and the Christian
family, but have enough experience to know that this is not always the
case. Running courses for parents and godparents and setting up
teams of visitors to support them are fuelled in part by an honest
desire to bring integrity to the sacrament, but they are also a response
to feelings of disappointment when so few make a connection
between the event and longer-term discipleship. They are fuelled, too,

by an attitude to sacraments which sees them as a possession of the Church only to be meted out to the worthy and faithful.

Others, particularly in more rural parishes, feel the weight of expectation from the local community where baptism has been administered on demand over the years. In some cases the relative infrequency of requests enables the minister to deal individually with every family but even this personal approach does not always bring improved commitment.

The availability of clerical and lay resources of time and talents may partially determine baptismal policy. For some parishes this will result in careful and lengthy preparation (especially where there are members of the Christian community with gifts in this area), but others, where there is a dearth of leaders and teachers, may have to acknowledge that resources need to be spread more widely and that educating families post-baptism may be more beneficial in the long run.

Treating people with care – relaxing into long-term ministry

Whatever the resources available for baptism preparation, it is essential to remember that those who seek baptism are not a homogeneous group; each of them comes with their own experience of the Church and of God. It is easy to assume that because they are not seen regularly in church they have no personal experience of God. This is clearly not true and, by assuming otherwise, far from preserving the integrity of the sacrament we simply demonstrate our own arrogance. Conversations with parents often show that they have thought carefully about faith. Church leaders need to tread carefully in order not to damage or deny the good experiences people have had in earlier encounters with God and his Church; nor should they suggest that God is only accessible through the church building or services but do everything they can to facilitate tenuous or dormant faith. At the same time, it is important to treat the sacrament with respect for God's grace is not cheap and members of the baptized community as well as enquirers need to hear this message.

If opportunities for contact are limited, it is all the more important to think about the way we use the time at our disposal and the attitude we and other members of our church should adopt. It is our strong contention that the best approach is to affirm what good experiences people have within them and whatever faith is already present and be honest about doubts and uncertainty.

When talking to parents and godparents, we sometimes use the image of scales, where one side represents the faith of the individual and the other their doubts. In speaking about the events in life that weigh down each pan of the scales people become more able to accept that few are without some faith and some doubts. The Church calls them to see these scales afresh and respond positively to the gift of baptism that is offered to their child. The image is a good analogy for how the collective faith of the worldwide Church can counter-balance the times of doubt within the life of the individual. There is no absolute faith within any individual or even within the Church; our hope rests in the person of Christ whose faith is ever sufficient.

In this postmodern age there are some who will disavow any faith and have scant knowledge of Christianity but this gives your church the opportunity of laying the first foundation-stone by your welcome, your attitude towards them and your honesty about the faith you and your congregation share. Do not expect a great response from such people; that joy will be for another Christian community in another place, perhaps many years from now. The nature of the mission of the Church is that the seeds we sow may well be watered by another and the harvest reaped by yet another. We cannot expect to see the whole picture instantly and we must rest content with that.

Many clergy give great care and attention to couples who come to church to be married. It is to be hoped that when they are settled and have children, the church they approach for baptism will build on the good foundations laid down; very often we shall be reawakening earlier good memories associated with Sunday School. At times, sadly, we shall be redressing bad memories and healing old wounds.

Through spouses, other family members, colleagues at work and friends, there are many opportunities for people to be guided towards the Church and a life built on faith. A welcoming response may ensure that people in the community have the confidence to approach the church, even if that confidence needs a long time to grow. People are well aware of the shortcomings of present-day life and its fractured relationships without the church making it harder still for them to come seeking God's touch and blessing for their children.

There are many opportunities to be pro-active in promoting baptism: major festivals, school assemblies, toddler clubs, the magazine – in fact, wherever the church and the community meet; and in reminding the whole congregation of their baptismal vocation. Easter Eve and Thanksgiving for Baptism services are ideal opportunities.

Seeing baptism in this way, as part of a lifelong process and the whole long-term ministry, may give us new perspectives about who we 'allow' to receive the sacrament.

Baptism and the existing Christian family

When a child or adult is baptized in the midst of the Christian community, it is a powerful reminder of the baptism that brought us into membership. It is a visual reminder that in our helplessness God brings gifts of cleansing, light and relationship, and a challenge to us to accept that the Christian family is dynamic and develops over time – which will stop us from stagnating into a tight and over-comfortable huddle.

We must make the baptism party welcome, be accommodating in our choice of hymns that day, simplify our liturgy and give out more instructions than regular members need. Much of this should happen before the service even begins. There is no reason these days to ask people to swap three times from one side of a card to another and then juggle two other books as well. A rehearsal before the day, to which godparents are also invited, shifts the awkwardness of a first entry into church. This itself helps visitors and hosts to be more relaxed with one another on the day and significantly improves the atmosphere.

Regular members should realize that everyone is valued and not expect to sit in the same seats they always do; but they should know when this will happen so that they can prepare and, if necessary, be educated as to why these things are important.

The baptism of teenagers and adults

Canon Law makes provision for the baptism of those who are 'of riper years' in Canon B24 by exhorting the minister to instruct the candidates in the principles of the faith and help them prepare by prayer and fasting. It points out that an adult should be confirmed as soon after baptism as possible.

> *1.   When any such person as is of riper years and able to answer for himself is to be baptized, the minister shall instruct such person, or cause him to be instructed, in the principles of the Christian religion, and exhort him so to prepare himself with prayers and fasting that he may receive this holy sacrament with repentance and faith.*

> *2.   At least a week before any such baptism is to take place, the minister shall give notice thereof to the bishop of the diocese or whomsoever he shall appoint for the purpose.*

> *3.   Every person thus baptised shall be confirmed by the bishop so soon after his baptism as conveniently may be; that so he may be admitted to the Holy Communion.*

If baptism is seen as one part of a cohesive ministry to the community, it is likely that there will be teenage and adult candidates coming forward. Some of these will be parents who, on bringing their own children for baptism, find themselves becoming involved in church activities, asking questions and regretting the fact that they were not baptized as infants. As one young woman said: 'I have never felt that I was God's child because I wasn't baptized.'

Weddings and funerals are also focal points for many people and at these times they will be sensitive to the call of God in their lives. This is happening more and more as people prefer to leave their children to make their own decisions later, so that adults coming to faith may start from a position of not having been baptized as children. It is hoped that they will move quickly on to confirmation but for some people one sacrament at a time is enough and they need time for reflection. It is good parish practice to give baptized adults a suitable book to enable such reflection to take place. Thus there are many new windows of opportunity opening which should be eagerly followed up. The new rite takes care that those old enough to answer for them-selves have particular parts to play in the service and are treated appropriately in order to acknowledge that this is an adult commit-ment with different connotations from infant baptism.

The baptism of those who are 'of riper years' requires a different approach from that of infants. It may be conducted by the bishop at a service of baptism and confirmation or take place in the normal baptismal liturgy of the local church. The liturgy makes clear that those old enough to speak up for themselves must do so and they are asked to declare their own commitment to worship and serve God.

Preparation will need to be more detailed and may be incorporated into an adult confirmation course. These candidates are a gift to the church; they come keen to be nurtured and educated and with few preconceived ideas, so there is little to unlearn. Occasionally, somebody presents themselves not knowing whether they were baptized as a baby and in this case the bishop or priest will use the conditional form of words '*If* you have not already been baptized...' Godparents are not necessary for adults but the church should provide sponsors who will give long-term support.

Facing rejection

However welcoming and positive the church is, we have to face the reality of disappointment and rejection. The Christian faith stands for commitment to community and loving service of others and these things can be costly. In the formality of worship, such rejection may be subdued, but the extent to which it is present above or below the surface will have an effect on the Christian community as it worships. It may be present in members of the congregation as well as in visitors and if responded to correctly can be a blessing to the church, for it brings the world into our worship and reminds people of the attitudes they experience in their daily lives.

Rejection can also be an opportunity to remind ourselves that Christianity is a threat and a challenge and that it elicits rejection in people as well as acceptance. Christ's experience should teach us the reality of that.

SECTION TWO

Baptism:
Preparing the Baptism Family
and Godparents

❹

BAPTISM PREPARATION

The initial contact

The phone rings. A voice – usually female, though not necessarily – says 'Is that the vicar? I'd like to arrange a baptism/book the church for a christening/make an appointment to see you/get my baby done next Sunday' or words to that effect. The exact nature of the opening gambit will depend on where you live and the culture of your community. In our parishes we meet the extremes: at one end of the spectrum (and the parish) are those who consider that the vicar exists solely to be their personal chaplain and expect no discussion about the date and time the baptism will take place; at the other end are those who are apologetic about troubling the vicar and are worried that their humble request will be refused because they live on the 'estate' or haven't been to church for ages.

Some requests are straightforward. Those who are regular members of the congregation will want to share this occasion with the church family; those who live within the parish boundaries have a right to baptism in their parish church, though many of them will not know that. Others living beyond the parish boundaries, who attend services sporadically or know the clergy through school, work or other occasional offices, will assume that they can have a baptism at their church; a few think they can choose the church or vicar of their dreams and book a baptism rather as they order a Chinese takeaway. Here Canon Law (under paragraph 5) gives clear guidelines. A minister who intends to baptize a child whose parents are living outside the boundaries of his/her care of souls and who does not have their names on the Church electoral roll 'shall not proceed to the baptism without having sought the good will of the minister of the parish in which such parents reside.'

Some will approach the church because they have been refused (or *feel* they have been refused) baptism in the parish in which they live and have heard that you might be sympathetic. If a parish imposes strict conditions of attendance on parents, they may feel that they must look elsewhere and they are disappointed if neighbouring churches are unable to meet their needs. All applicants in this category should be aware that, if the minister of the first parish is in fact refusing to baptize the child or allow him/her to be baptized in another parish, the proper course is for parents to apply to the bishop.

There are parents who want to bring the baby 'home' to the church where they grew up or where their parents now live. In these circumstances there needs to be a discussion about the meaning of the baptism and the importance of belonging to a local community (church or otherwise). When encouraged to make contact with their own church to find out more, they may be welcomed into the fold and opt for a local service, especially if the pressure has come from the grandparents, as is sometimes the case. It is infinitely preferable that links are made where they live so that the child and family can be nurtured and provided for. If they are determined to keep up the family tradition of baptisms at the parental home, they must seek their own incumbent's blessing so that he or she has details of the family and can follow up the contact.

Overall, a careful balance needs to be struck between providing ideal Christian nurture and not discounting the importance to a person of their feelings of loyalty and attachment to a particular place. It is important to remember that some new parents do not grow away from their own parents and continue to be supported and directed by them.

Whatever the circumstances of the request, all those involved in the initial contact should be aware that the response they make will colour the relationship from then on. Enquirers come with several sub-texts running beneath an apparently innocent and uncomplicated request, but the need for acceptance and positive affirmation is universal. A negative response – even if only conveyed in the tone of voice – will suggest to parents that you, ergo the Church, ergo God, are not interested in their child or them, or that they are second-class people. The unspoken question: 'Is the church (God) for us or against us, even though we haven't been to church for years/don't say our prayers/are divorced/a single parent/not married, etc., etc?' will be there. The reproduction of children and their consequent protection is one of the most powerful drives in the human psyche, and clergy, secretaries and administrators need to have this firmly in mind before they open their mouths when they hear the words 'Is that the vicar?'

For some, one visit will be arranged and then a convenient date found; for others there will be a list of questions to be answered satisfactorily, ranging from 'Why do you want your baby baptized?' to 'What do you understand to be the crux of Romans 6?'. The advent of the new liturgy may be a good time to consider the kind of preparation required for parents, godparents and the congregation, so that everybody understands the service and the nature of Christian faith and discipleship.

Level 1 preparation

Churches differ in the way they follow up the initial enquiry. Some clergy may be content with only one meeting, which may take place in the family home or on church premises. The content of the interview may be wide-ranging, from 'Isn't your baby beautiful?' to 'Why do you want Johnny baptized?', but will serve to allay anxieties, build relationships and make further communication both positive and possible. Such discussion should always be sensitive to building on where the parents are rather than where they might be in an ideal world. The art of listening to the parents' story of faith, however short and insignificant it may seem to be, is an art worth acquiring. Imparting knowledge or teaching should be the second phase rather than the initial one.

These meetings can be interpreted by sceptics as reconnaissance by the Church to decide whether the baby qualifies, or they can be experienced as genuine opportunities to get to know one another, exercise pastoral care and answer questions. For some churches, this will be the extent of the preparation and they will move quickly on to discussing practicalities and arranging the date. This may be the time to leave a copy of the *Baptism* and *Becoming a Godparent* leaflets.[1]

Level 2 preparation

Other churches have a rather more complex response to an initial baptism enquiry. Here, the Level 1 meeting is purely exploratory – a getting-to-know-you session that is followed by a longer session with the clergy or other members of the congregation. Here are two descriptions of such an approach:

> *I have a meeting in which I explain the essential meaning of baptism, the requirements for godparents and give details of the application form and a leaflet for them to read. No date is discussed yet. Then the couple see two Pastoral Assistants who have done training in baptism preparation, go through the service in detail and watch the CPAS video* Stairway. *The option of a Thanksgiving Service is discussed but if parents are happy to go ahead with baptism, dates are discussed.*[2]

> *An initial visit is made by the parish priest to establish contact and to fill in the baptism application form. The priest makes a subsequent visit to discuss the meaning of baptism and to show a video of a baptism being celebrated at St Nicolas in the context of the Parish Mass so as to explain what happens and why. A lay person from a small group of Baptism Befrienders will also visit just before the baptism.*[3]

Even one or two visits provide quite an opportunity for preparation, but they are clearly not sufficient to complete a full Christian initiation course. The ministry team needs to be clear about its aims in this minimalist preparation, which may involve some or all of the following:

- establishing a working relationship;

- allaying fears and anxieties;

- ensuring that practicalities are clearly explained;

- providing information about other church activities;

- brief discussions about belonging to the Church (local and worldwide), the pilgrimage of faith, the Christian lifestyle;

- a walk and talk through the contents of the service.

This kind of preparation can and should be done by lay members of the congregation as well as clergy and often provides a basis for new relationships to be formed, especially where those involved have children of a similar age. The importance placed on the congregation in the liturgy underlines the importance of using them in every aspect of baptismal work: preparation, worship and post-baptismal follow-up.

Level 3 preparation

Some will feel that the kind of preparation offered above is inadequate and that parents need to be much more knowledgeable and committed before their children are allowed to be baptized. Such parishes might require attendance at an Alpha, Emmaus or other Christian Basics course to ensure understanding of the faith and the Bible. In addition, they will want to be sure that the family is committed to church attendance, which can only be proved over a period of time.

Some parishes write their own material and use lay people and clergy to deliver this in church or house groups. Others choose to incorporate potential baptism parents into the wider educational programme of the church so that they study alongside other interested enquirers. Either way, more material will be covered and more instruction given than in Levels 1 and 2. This assumes that baptism is the *result* of some kind of training, rather than the beginning; but it also ensures that all concerned can participate in the service with integrity.

In addition to the topics covered at Level 2, a whole range of matters might be included, such as:

- Who is God? What do we think/feel about him? What does the Bible/Christian experience show us?

- Who is Jesus? What was he like? What did he do and teach?

- Why are Jesus' death and resurrection so important? What do they tell us about us and God and how the world works?

- Who is the Holy Spirit? How does the Spirit help us in our Christian life?

- How can we begin to read the Bible so that it is a valuable resource in our lives?

- How can we develop our life of prayer and become holy people?

- What are sacraments? Why are baptism and communion so important for the Christian life?

- Why is it important to belong to the Church and worship God?

Opinion is divided regarding the merits of imposing conditions upon prospective baptism families. Some of them are frightened away or feel rejected by having what they perceive to be severe restrictions placed upon them; others, having been required to undertake a course of study, are led to make a firm commitment to Jesus Christ and the Church. Similarly, some of those who find baptism freely available will be moved to find out more while others will treat it as a right and never be seen again. There is no clear evidence to suggest that either method produces more committed Christians in the long run. Our practice is to ensure that those who approach us feel that they are allowed to belong to the Christian community before their belief is put to the test, not least because this is often the pattern for other members of the congregation. We would therefore advocate extended Christian teaching programmes *after* the person has been welcomed into the life of the church. In the end, however, parishes and clergy must remain true to their own integrity and do what they think is right.

Baptism visitors

Every parish should have regular members of the congregation who will undertake the work of befriending baptism families and sharing in the preparation for and administration of the baptism and any visits after the service. Some parishes like to use couples with young children who will have much in common with other parents, but often older people are helpful in fulfilling pseudo-parental roles, especially in an increasingly mobile population where families live far apart from one another. This role is destined to become even more significant in the light of the new liturgy, with its new emphasis on the role of the church community in the sacrament of baptism.

Offering a caring, Christian relationship

Finally, it is important to acknowledge people come with histories of faith and no faith; hope and no hope. There may be relationship problems, difficulties at work, homelessness or overcrowding, any of which can drown out the voice of the church, even as baptism is sought. (It is good practice to ask if there are current anxieties or recent bereavements in the family, and to include these in the prayers during the service.) Offering friendship and Christian love each and every time the phone rings or the doorbell goes is an act which of itself builds the kingdom of God most effectively. And as a consequence it is the hardest work we have to do. It requires us to set aside the times we have felt used or had our hopes dashed and to forget the inconvenience of the call in order to treat the latest enquiry with a warm smile and a new hope in Christ.

5

GODPARENTS

What are godparents for?

In the past, godparents have fulfilled two major roles: as additional members of the extended family providing support and care, and as sponsors for baptism. These roles still hold true but a common misconception in the minds of parents is that godparents automatically become legal guardians, which is not so (though guardians and godparents may be the same people). The new liturgy reinforces the pre-Reformation view that godparents become part of the family, by asking quite specifically whether they 'will care for them and help them to take their place within the life and worship of Christ's Church'.[1]

Most people are delighted to be asked because it suggests they are valued and trusted friends. What they do not always understand is that a godparent should be a good example of Christian living, relied upon to pray for the child, speak to them of God and encourage them in their Christian faith as they grow up and come to confirmation. So some churches provide godparents with a *Becoming a Godparent* leaflet[2] to read before the baptism. This explains to them why they are being asked and what is expected of them in an ideal world. This leaflet is also helpful in giving guidance to parents regarding the choice of godparents when they have not already made their decision. In addition, parents might be asked to give them a letter, samples of which are on pp. 44–5. These can be photocopied and adapted to the needs of individual parishes and localities.

Canon B23 Of godparents and sponsors

1.   For every child to be baptized there shall be not fewer than three godparents, of whom at least two shall be of the same sex as the child and of whom at least one shall be of the opposite sex; save that, when three cannot conveniently be had, one godfather and godmother shall suffice. Parents may be godparents for their own children provided that the child have at least one other god-parent. [NB: they should be named as such.]

2.   The godparents shall be persons who will faithfully fulfil their responsibilities both by their care for the children committed to their charge and by the example of their own godly living.

3.   When one who is of riper years is to be baptised he shall choose three, or at least two, to be his sponsors, who shall be ready to present him at the font and afterwards put him in mind of his Christian profession and duties.

4.   No person shall be admitted to be a sponsor or godparent who has not been baptized and confirmed. Nevertheless the minister shall have power to dispense with the requirement of confirmation in any case in which in his judgement need so requires. [NB: there is no minimum age stipulated.]

Who may be a godparent?

Canon Law (Canon B23) requires the godparents to be people who will faithfully fulfil their responsibilities, both by their care for the child and by 'the example of their own godly living'. They must be baptized and must normally be confirmed, although the member of the clergy concerned may dispense witht the requirement of confirmation in a particular case if he or she considers it necessary to do so. Provided these legal requirements are satisfied, the parents have the right to choose whoever they wish to be the godparents. It used to be easier to find godparents who fulfilled these requirements but increasingly (depending on the nature of the parish) those in their twenties and thirties are not confirmed and may not even be baptized. This leaves the family and the church with something of a problem. Favourite brothers, sisters and friends find they are disenfranchised before they have even begun; on the other hand, this is a prime opportunity to invite them along to an enquirers' course so that they can make their own commitment before becoming a godparent.

Whom to choose

Canon Law requires that a child should have three godparents, at least two of whom are the same sex as the child, but when 'three cannot conveniently be had, one godfather and one godmother shall suffice'. There is some sense in this; even in these days of political correctness boys still want and need to relate to men and girls to women. However, this is not an absolutely hard and fast rule; there can be only one godmother and one godfather, or there can be only one extra godparent if the parents choose to fulfil this role themselves, but in this case the parents should specifically agree to be godparents.

It is good to encourage parents to think carefully about who will be godparents and how many there will be. Some ministers will give them some or all of the following advice:

- Do not choose grandparents. Grandparents will necessarily be older than the parents and may not see the child to maturity. More importantly, they will be fulfilling a loving, caring role as grandparents and if they are Christian will be providing an example of godly living through all their contacts with the child. Other godparents will provide additional adults to help in this task.

- Do not stand as godparents yourselves. Where parents are providing Christian examples and bringing their children up 'to walk in the ways of Christ', they can only be helped in this by having additional significant adults with special responsibilities. As children move into adolescence they may find it easier to talk to people other than their parents about matters of faith and spirituality, and to keep such an important task as a preserve of the parents is to confuse the roles and diminish the opportunities for adult input provided for the child. Statistics suggest that the number of marriages which fail is high; should there be family difficulties it may be godparents who provide some stability and support.

- Do not concede to family pressures to ask brothers and sisters to be godparents just because 'it is their turn' or they assume it is their right. Aunts, uncles and close relatives will have a special relationship already and, if they are not able to provide Christian guidance, should not be asked automatically.

- Do not have more than four godparents. Parents may wish to ask two couples, which makes sense, but more than four can mean that godparents lose their uniqueness and rely on the others to do the job.

- Godparents are very important people and, if chosen well, can have an enormous influence for good.

Preparing godparents

As we have seen, churches vary in their preparation of parents before baptism but most have at least one meeting or rehearsal for parents. Godparents may be invited to attend as well, where practical, and this is an ideal opportunity to address them specifically about the nature of the commitment they are to make. Where they are unable to be present before the day, the leaflet *Godparents* is ideal to send them in advance via parents so that they can be well prepared, together with a letter, simple examples of which are given at the end of this chapter.

When godparents can't be present

Obviously, godparents make every effort to be present but if this is impossible through sickness or because they are living abroad, somebody else can act as proxy for them on the day. Wherever they are, it may be possible for them to visit a local church to pray for their godchild and to say the promises at the same time as they are being said back home. Few godparents think of this possibility and so it is good to recommend it to them as an alternative.

Godparent cards

These are cards which we strongly commend to ministers. They give details of the baptism and a reminder of the promises which have been made. They may be presented at the end of the service with the suggestion that they are not put in a file for safe keeping but displayed at home or work in a prominent place such as a kitchen or study noticeboard. If godparents remember their godchildren and ask God to bless them every time they pass by the card they will be fulfilling at least one of their functions regularly. Godparents may appreciate an up-to-date photo of their godchild to put with the card; this in itself is a way of keeping in contact in an age of mobility.

The card is also a reminder of the date of baptism so that they can mark it like a birthday with a card or small present. This means that godparents are easily distinguishable from other relatives and friends and it makes the event notable. They may be encouraged to talk or write to their godchildren about their faith, send copies of favourite

41

prayers and take an interest in important life-events so that children see that God is interested in them as real people in every facet of life.

At confirmation

When young people (and even adults) come for confirmation, we encourage them to invite their godparents to the service which will not mark the end of the relationship but certainly be an important turning point. This is quite difficult in dioceses where confirmations happen midweek but in this event we suggest that godparents pray for their godchild at the time they know the service is taking place and visit as soon after as possible so that they can share communion together.

Sponsors

Sponsors and godparents are very similar. The Church recognizes both: sponsors in their role supporting baptism candidates; and godparents, who take on this role specifically for children. The title 'sponsor' may be preferred when the person to be baptized is an older child or adult who does not wish to have a godparent. In the new liturgy, the sponsor is one who has agreed 'to support in the journey of faith candidates of any age for baptism'.[3]

The sponsor can be chosen by the family but may be a member of the church congregation who agrees to take a special interest in that individual. Some non-Anglican churches assume that individual godparents are unnecessary because the whole church community will 'sponsor' children who come for baptism. This may be possible where numbers are small but, in reality, it may mean that nobody takes responsibility because they are relying on everybody else to do so.

Presents

If godparents ask for advice about presents for baptism and confirmation, it is best to stress that their presence and prayers are most important, rather than expensive gifts, but that it is right to mark the occasion of baptism or confirmation by giving something special. Godparents should not feel that they have to buy lavish presents; simple, meaningful gifts will be appreciated and mean more. One decision is whether to buy something for the baby to use now or something to be kept for later.

Here are some suggestions for presents to give godchildren at the time of baptism or confirmation:

- Bibles (there are a number of editions specifically for children).

- Books of prayers: a wide variety for all ages is available from all good Christian bookshops and if you have a church bookstall it should stock a representative sample if you conduct many baptisms. This will encourage people to buy them who might not take the time to find a Christian bookshop – and also add to your income!

- Small wooden crosses.

- A silver or gold cross and chain.

- An inscribed paperweight in marble/stone from a specialist engraver. These often have the fish symbol, a cross, the initial of the child or the date of the baptism.

- Drawings, paintings or posters of Christian stories – art galleries or cathedral bookshops are good places to find these.

- A nativity or crib set.

Sample letters to godparents – to be sent before the baptism

A. St Erkenwald's by the Sea

Dear Godparent,

Congratulations on becoming a godparent. I'm sure you're delighted to have been asked, but it's also a responsibility and you may be wondering what's expected of you. Baptism is a service of commitment to Jesus Christ. In the baptism service godparents are asked if they are willing to help their god-child by their prayers, by their example and by their teaching. You will also be asked to declare that you reject the devil, renounce evil and repent of your sins and to state that you turn to Christ, submit to him and come to him as the way, the truth and the life.

Some godparents will not have had the opportunity to think through these promises in detail and it does sound rather a lot to do, so if you are unsure about what it all means, please contact us or your own parish priest.

The most important thing to understand is that you are promising to seek God's support in your own life, to follow Jesus Christ's teaching to the best of your ability and to ask God's forgiveness when you fail. You make the promises for yourself and as a sign of your willingness to support your god-child in their Christian life.

To help you further, we have a rehearsal for parents and godparents in church on .... at .... to explain what will happen on the day and talk about what baptism means. You are warmly invited to this meeting, but we will understand if it is not practical for you to attend; the enclosed leaflet gives you more information.

At the baptism itself we will give you a special card in the name of your god-child. We suggest that you don't put this away in a drawer for safe keeping but keep it on display. It can then act as a reminder for you to think of your godchild as they grow up and ask God to bless them daily.

With very best wishes,

B. St Ogg's Church, Church Street

Dear Godparent,

You must be very pleased to have been asked to be a godparent. It means that your friends or relations hope you will take a real interest in their child and be a good example of Christian living. If you have any questions about what being a godparent means or the promises you will be asked to make, please give me a ring so that we can discuss them.

I am enclosing a leaflet about godparents so that you can read more fully about what you are agreeing to do.

I look forward to seeing you at church for the baptism and, if you are able to come, at the rehearsal in church on ....

With all good wishes,

Some prayers for godparents

These may be used during the service or reproduced without permission and given to godparents.

A PRAYER FOR YOUR GODCHILD

Heavenly Father,
thank you for the gift of *Rachel*
and for all the joy *she* brings us.
Be with *her* on *her* Christian journey
so that *she* may come to know you
as *her* saviour and her friend.
Amen.

A PRAYER FOR GODPARENTS

Lord God,
I pray that you will guide and support me
in being a godparent.
Give me your wisdom and your love,
help me to be a good example of Christian living,
and keep me mindful of my duties.
Amen.

Godparents are extremely important people in the spiritual nurture of children and young people, and it is hoped that they will be given attention, instruction and support as far as possible. Even if the godparents of the children baptized in your church come from far-flung places, why not consider giving an occasional reminder to those of the congregation who have godchildren elsewhere about their duties and responsibilities. This can be as simple as referring to all godparents during any baptism service when the declarations are made by the parents and godparents of the moment. In this way, they will be made aware that all godparents hold a position of influence and responsibility which should not be taken lightly.

SECTION THREE

Baptism:
The Service

6

THE BAPTISM SERVICE: USING THE NEW LITURGY

Baptism is part of an integrated process of Christian initiation rather than an isolated event in the life of one individual. Initiation does not end with the baptism service; rather, this is the beginning of a lifelong process and the liturgy makes this very clear.[1] Therefore, there are some important changes in emphasis which, although not novel, give a different flavour and feel to the rite. It is these which we shall be exploring in this chapter.

When should we baptize?

The contents page of the service book gives several alternatives for the conduct of baptism. It may occur at the Eucharist or separately, with confirmation, at Morning or Evening Prayer, or at a Service of the Word. The structure of the service means that it contains sufficient material of substance for it to stand independently as a worthwhile act of worship; this may be appropriate and advisable at certain times and places, although it has implications for the place of the local congregation in the liturgy.

However, the aim of the liturgy and the Church's understanding of the theology of baptism require that, wherever possible, baptism should take place in the presence of the main congregation. Certainly, it should never be seen as a private ceremony conducted at the whim of one family in time for a civilized afternoon tea. It is a public service and part of the liturgy of the Church of England. Perhaps this is especially important in an age where, for many, there is little sense of community as families are scattered and mobile, and the parish church is no longer the centre of village life.

The structure of the service

The service outline has four sections: Preparation, the Liturgy of the Word, the Liturgy of Baptism and Commission. In a eucharistic context, the Liturgy of the Eucharist follows the Liturgy of Baptism.

Preparation comprises a greeting, an optional thanksgiving prayer, an apologetic for baptism which draws together the major theological themes, and a collect which highlights the activity of God in the present ('you give your faithful people new life') and the future hope ('that we may grow into the full stature of your Son, Jesus Christ').

Then follows the Liturgy of the Word: a psalm or canticle, two or three readings and the sermon. There are clear directions in the Notes which follow the service outline about which collects and readings should be used on any particular day. Those provided in Appendix 5 are particularly for services where baptism is the predominant element.

The Liturgy of Baptism begins with the presentation of the candidates, general questions to the congregation, parents and godparents, more detailed questions entitled 'Decision' and the signing of the cross on the forehead of each candidate with the accompanying familiar prayer.

At this stage, the ministers and candidates move to the font if necessary, where a prayer over the water is said followed by the congregational profession of faith. Then follows the threefold baptism by sprinkling or immersion and a short prayer. The party leaves the font at this point.

The Commission sums up what has taken place in the service and provides space for intercessions and the Lord's Prayer. There are special sections for the newly baptized who are old enough to answer for themselves and the climax is the Welcome and Peace, after which lighted candles are given to all candidates as they are sent out into the world 'in the light and peace of Christ'.

If the Eucharist is to follow, the service follows the same pattern as above but after the Welcome and Peace moves into the normal Liturgy of the Eucharist, differentiated only by the proper preface and optional post-communion prayer.

The Commentary by the Liturgical Commission at the end of the service book gives more detailed advice and instruction about the nature of the rites and the rationale for the work of revision. This commentary should be read by all those engaged in practical ministry and not seen as optional reading material.

The new emphases

Within the structure outlined above, there are some emphases inter-woven throughout the liturgy. These are not original but their importance is underlined through the new rites.

1   THE PLACE OF THE PEOPLE OF GOD

In this new liturgy, one notable feature is an explicit emphasis on the importance of the congregation – the local church community repre-senting the worldwide communion – into which the child is to be baptized. In the past, the congregation joined in the prayer of welcome and made responses in particular parts of the service (the giving of the candle and the declaration of faith), but their role, both during the service and afterwards, is now very firmly underlined, stressing the corporate nature of belonging and the community 'own-ership' of the candidates and their families. It is to the congregation, rather than to the parents and godparents, that the first questions are addressed and it is their presence which gives validity to the sacra-ment of baptism.

The service must therefore be embraced as a corporate, family occasion having repercussions not only on the families themselves but on the whole People of God. Baptism families are not to be seen as (at worst) impostors to be tolerated or (at best) visitors to be smiled at and then forgotten. The regular congregation is called upon to take responsibility and be more than polite bystanders.

At the beginning of the Liturgy of Baptism, the People of God are asked quite clearly to welcome the new members of the church and they reaffirm this at the exchange of the Peace: 'In baptism the Lord is adding to our number those whom he is calling. People of God, will you welcome these children and uphold them in their new life in Christ?' The minister also tells parents and godparents in a quite uncompromising way that 'the Church receives these children with joy'. This is an unconditional statement in the present tense – not a possibility or a vain hope for some unspecified time in the future.

After the baptism, the assembled company is addressed by the minister, who says: '*We* have brought these children to baptism . . . *We* have prayed that in Jesus Christ they will know the forgiveness of their sins and the new life of the Spirit.' The act has been a communal one, focused, it is true, on the will of the parents and godparents but embracing the whole body of the church.

The minister goes on to say that 'they [the children] will need the help and encouragement of the Christian community' and that 'we all have a duty to support them by prayer, example and teaching'. It is not sufficient that the parents and godparents have done what is necessary for their child to be baptized. It is also vital that those already within the church should be clear about their task in relation to its newest and perhaps most vulnerable members. The congregation are asked to affirm their faith together with the candidates because it is the 'faith of the Church' – not mine or yours alone. Thereby, both parents and congregation acknowledge publicly their commitment to one another in a way which is far more explicit than before. This strikes a balance between the specific duties of the parents and godparents and the equally important duties of the congregation. Families should be made to feel that they will be supported and encouraged by the local church in what is a difficult and lifelong task; and the local church may need reminding from time to time of the declarations and promises it has made with regard to the children whom it has welcomed into its fellowship 'with joy'.

This whole emphasis may make it easier for ministers who are reluctant to baptize children of parents whose faith is perceived to be deficient or inadequate in some way. Those who are hesitant about the efficacy of baptism in these cases might be persuaded to take a less prescriptive view, because the faith of the community is as important as that of the individual and may make up for the inadequacies of any parent(s) who brings a child along for baptism. Within the 'faith of the Church', 'we' who have brought these children to baptism will find ample faith to sustain belief.

And even for those parents who come with a professed and firm faith, there is the surety and added confidence that they do not bear the burden alone. Where they are weak, the church may be strong; when they struggle with their lifelong task of bringing up the child 'to walk in the ways of Christ', the church will be there to encourage and uphold them. When they fail, there will be others to redress the balance.

This new emphasis has particular consequences for baptism services that do not take place during normal Sunday worship. While 'private baptism' is to be strongly discouraged, parishes do often hold baptism services at which the regular congregation is not present, and the new liturgy does provide for a 'Service of the Word' which is not the main Sunday act of worship. There are advantages in this practice.

Families with very little knowledge of Christian faith and worship need not be 'forced' into services that make them feel inadequate and isolated at an important moment in the life of their child; Sunday worship is not overwhelmed by the sacrament of baptism (one of our parishes baptizes 70 children each year); and, if taken seriously, baptism services that stand alone can have a real sense of corporate worship about them. We commend the practice of bringing several families together (though not more than four), the singing of hymns, an appropriate talk and, wherever possible, the presence of a number from the regular congregation.

It is possible that the new liturgy will encourage more clergy to ask members of the regular congregation to be present in an official capacity at such services and to make the responses accordingly (perhaps with members of other churches who are baptismal party guests). For, although the new importance given to the congregation may be theologically sound, it does provide practical problems for churches which have specific baptism services. The service book states that baptism may take place within Morning or Evening Prayer or a Service of the Word but in practice it may be unlikely that the majority of regular worshippers will be present at these. Thus, careful thought needs to be given to how the questions addressed to the congregation may be answered with integrity if they are not in attendance.

2   A PILGRIM PEOPLE

Another aspect which is stressed in the new liturgy is the idea of the journey or pilgrimage of faith. Research into faith development has shown that most Christians come to faith gradually and that their growth and learning takes place as if on a slow incline rather than as a dramatic event. It has shown also that a greater number of Christians reach adult faith through the influence of their friends, family and other close adults than through major evangelistic ventures. The 'Road to Damascus' style of conversion experiences, though well documented, should not be seen as the primary way to come to faith.

In Chapter 2 we explored whether baptism should come before or after the reception of faith. For those who would say that absolute, unhesitant, undeniable faith is a prerequisite for baptism, the journey comes first; but others say that the experience of baptism is one part of the whole journey and that faith of a different kind is given continually afterwards. Thus, even the most unconfident baptism enquirer has some faith which should be acknowledged and nurtured. The Church may have been guilty of extinguishing the flickering flames of faith imparted by friends and family over the years with an ill-timed rejection – or what is perceived as rejection.

The new liturgy implies that the giving of the sacrament is part of a pilgrimage package which will continue throughout the whole of life, and that faith in Christ is not a once-for-all event but something which grows and changes in the same way that individuals develop in other areas of life. Thus the baby learns to roll over, crawl, stand up, toddle and then run in some kind of natural progression. The potential for running the marathon is present in the newborn baby though nobody would actually expect her to be able to do it. Similarly, the potential for adult faith is present in the experience of the infant.

Thus the collect prays that we may 'grow into the full stature of your Son, Jesus Christ'; parents and godparents are asked to '[trust] God for their growth in faith' and are told: 'In baptism these children begin their journey in faith.' Immediately after the administration of the water, the minister prays for the candidates, that they may be daily renewed 'within the company of Christ's pilgrim people'. Most explicitly, the optional address to those 'old enough to understand' spells out this idea:

Today God has touched you with his love
and given you a place among his people.
God promises to be with you
in joy and in sorrow,
to be your guide in life,
and to bring you safely to heaven.
In baptism God invites you on a life-long journey.
Together with all God's people
you must explore the way of Jesus
and grow in friendship with God,
in love for his people,
and in serving others.
With us you will listen to the word of God
and receive the gifts of God.

A prayer which speaks of God as one who 'promises to be with you in joy and in sorrow, to be your guide in life' and who 'invites you on a life-long journey' in which 'you must explore the way of Jesus and grow in friendship with God' quite clearly acknowledges that the newly baptized (or their parent(s)) do not come to baptism with all the answers to faith neatly resolved. It gives permission for uncertainty, questioning and doubts which will be faced honestly and openly along the path of faith with the support of others engaged on the same pilgrimage. This is a welcome and refreshing image and one which will encourage many.

But this idea of pilgrimage should not be used to suggest that baptism is merely an inferior first stage on a journey which will become more meaningful, real and adult as the child grows to maturity. The Anglican Communion recognizes that baptism is effective immediately and is for the present as well as for the future; baptized infants are as much a part of the Church by right as are their adult counterparts.

3   MORE CHALLENGING QUESTIONS

After the presentation of the candidates, the Liturgy of Baptism continues with a series of questions and responses for parents and god-parents or those old enough to answer for themselves. They are similar in content to those asked in earlier liturgies, though in a slightly different order. The first three involve a turning away from all that is negative:

> *Do you reject the devil and all rebellion against God?*
> **I reject them.**
> *Do you renounce the deceit and corruption of evil?*
> **I renounce them.**
> *Do you repent of the sins that separate us from God and neighbour?*
> **I repent of them.**

The second three involve a positive turning towards Christ.

> *Do you turn to Christ as Saviour?*
> **I turn to Christ.**
> *Do you submit to Christ as Lord?*
> **I submit to Christ.**
> *Do you come to Christ, the way, the truth and the life?*
> **I come to Christ.**

There is a choice of prayers for infants or those old enough to answer for themselves and a further series of questions covering both the private and public face of commitment for those who are old enough to answer for themselves. They ask whether they will 'continue in the apostles' teaching and fellowship', 'persevere in resisting evil', 'proclaim . . . the good news', 'seek and serve Christ' and 'acknowledge Christ's authority'. There should be no doubt, then, that there are firm and different expectations placed upon those who receive baptism as adults.

The symbols of the liturgy

Perhaps more than any other act of worship, baptism services lend themselves most obviously to symbolic experience. Although the appropriate words explain the meaning of the theology behind them, the symbols do, in fact, speak for themselves and should be allowed to do so. They remain the same: water, light, clothing, oil and the sign of the cross, and options are given for the order in which they appear, whether or not they are to be used at all and the stress placed upon each of them.

1   CANDLES

Light is the most obvious and easily understood symbol for baptism, since human fear of the dark and welcoming of the dawn are set deep within the human psyche. Many churches use the special Paschal candle, with all its reminders of Easter, at any service where a baptism takes place. This candle has the advantage of being large and visible. In the new liturgy, it is lit immediately before the statement: 'In baptism, God calls us out of darkness into his marvellous light', which leads into the first set of questions addressed to parents and godparents.

The two sets of three questions mirror this statement: the first series demands a rejection of darkness and the second invites a response to all that is light (as represented by Christ). A turning away and turning around are envisaged here – underlining the meaning of repentance as repositioning, facing another way. In *Children in the Church?* the writers suggest that the congregation might be asked to face the back of the church, which is in darkness, and then literally turn towards the light as a reminder that this is what baptism is all about.

Unlike the old liturgy, the individual lighted candles which are to be taken home are given at the very end of the service after the Blessing and are accompanied by short, relevant statements and commissions. The candle reminds the baptized that they are one with 'the saints in light', that they must 'walk in this light', 'shine as a light' and 'Go in the light and peace of Christ'. Baptism is outward-looking, then, and offers something to the wider world as well as to the individual recipient.

Baptism candles are a vital reminder for many families and there are various types available from all major Christian suppliers. Some stand in a card base, others have plastic boxes, but whichever you choose they are a necessary prerequisite. Months or years later, when the family brings another baby for baptism, older brothers and sisters enjoy bringing their own candles back to church to be relit. Parents can be advised to keep the candles and relight them on the anniversary of their child's baptism as reminders to them and the children of what has been promised and received.

2   THE SIGN OF THE CROSS

As early as the second century, Christians were using the 'sign of the Lord' in order to sanctify everything they did throughout the day from waking to sleeping; it was partly a reminder to themselves to keep them on the straight and narrow and partly a sign of recognition for fellow pilgrims, especially in times of trouble and persecution. It became a regular feature of baptism and confirmation and remains so today. In infant baptism, the baby does not, of course, sign himself but the priest makes the sign on his or her forehead and may invite the godparents and sponsors to do the same. This is an invisible but indelible mark of sanctity, belonging and unity with Christ crucified.

In the new liturgy, this happens before the actual baptism but after the lighting of the large candle. When all have been signed, these words are spoken: 'Do not be ashamed to confess the faith of Christ crucified.' The cross unites the baptized with the death of Christ and links them irrevocably to him. For those who are concerned in principle about using the sign of the cross, Canon B25 explains that it has been retained in the baptism service 'in remembrance of the Cross, which is very precious to those that believe in Jesus Christ', and also points out that this follows the practice of the early Church.

3   OIL FOR ANOINTING (COMMONLY KNOWN AS CHRISM)

The priests and kings of the Old Testament were often anointed with oil[3] and this practice was adopted by the early Church, although there is no major New Testament evidence for its use apart from the anointing of Jesus' feet by the woman in the Pharisee's house.[4] The Fathers attest to its use at baptism and confirmation services (as well as at ordination and holy unction) and these are two of the sacraments where it is still used in some traditions. Anointing with oil is by no means obligatory, and local tradition and churchmanship will often determine its use. The rubrics state that pure olive oil consecrated by the bishop should be used and that its use reminds us of athletes preparing for a contest who use it to give them strength. Such oil may be used to sign the child, but other oil mixed with fragrant spices may accompany the prayer which follows the threefold administration. This demonstrates the 'blessings of the messianic era and the richness of the Holy Spirit'.

4   WATER

Water plays a crucial part in the physical life of the world. Without it, the creation could not be sustained and the effects of a prolonged absence of water are quite clearly evident. Life without it leads inevitably to death; but it is not physical life alone which requires water. For spiritual health, it is necessary to be washed and cleansed by God. In the Old Testament, religious purity necessitated many ritual washings in order to keep the people holy and as a counter to the 'uncleanness' of the Gentiles. This ritual washing was not enough on its own, however, and there were frequent injunctions to make the inner man as clean as the outer. The act of physical cleansing would have little effect if the person continued to be inwardly evil, but external and internal activities were always closely related.

The prayer over the water explains the history and significance of water in some detail – it sustains, refreshes and cleanses all life and the analogy between physical washing and spiritual cleansing is made clear in a way which will be accessible to most people. The water is water of purification because it makes holy and cleanses the whole person in a way which ordinary water cannot; it is life-giving because without it we are dead; it brings the Holy Spirit.[5]

In the new rite, the profession of faith by the whole congregation has been inserted between the blessing of the water and the administration of baptism, as if to provide a check that the theology of salvation expounded in the prayer over the water is what the people really believe. The trinitarian baptismal formula remains the same.

Sometimes, parents ask whether they may add to the water of baptism some 'holy' water which has been brought back from holidays in the Holy Land. The River Jordan, they think, must have something special about it if Jesus was baptized there. It is our practice to accommodate such requests on the grounds that it would be churlish to refuse, but we are careful to point out that this does not make the baptism of their child superior to any other and that the physical source of the water is irrelevant. However, it provides a good link in their minds between the baptism of Jesus and that of their infant.

5   WHITE CLOTHES

Scripture and tradition suggest that the pure in heart will be recognized by their white clothes[6] and adult candidates may be symbolically clothed in white garments before full immersion. Practice varies among families bringing infants; many use the family heirloom handed down from generation to generation, which is invariably white or cream, while others prefer to dress their children (especially boys) in ordinary clothes. One family opted for full immersion of the baby (in a baby bath because the font was too small) and only afterwards was the child dressed in dry white clothes symbolic of regeneration and cleansing. The new services provide an optional place for a white robe to be put on after the baptism.

The post-baptismal commission

Following the custom of the BCP, this follows the baptism and is addressed to the congregation, parents and godparents. This serves to underline what has been the implicit and explicit message of the liturgy – that the act of baptism is part of an outworking of God's gracious activity rather than something given after all the conditions have been met. It is part of the process of salvation, forgiveness and newness of life rather than the result of those things. So we pray 'that in Jesus Christ they will know the forgiveness of their sins and the new life of the Spirit'.

The baptism of 'those old enough to answer for themselves'

It is still true that the majority of baptisms taking place in the Church of England are for babies and infants brought by their parents. The number of adults and teenagers being baptized is, however, on the increase and reflects a changing attitude to infant baptism. The rites take this into account and are clear that such people should participate fully and actively in the service rather than seeing baptism as something which is done to them.

At the presentation of candidates, the president asks them whether they want to be baptized and they may give a testimony if they wish. They will answer the questions themselves when it comes to the

Decision and will be asked to affirm that they accept the faith of the Church with the words 'This is my faith'. The president may address the candidates after baptism at the section beginning 'today God has touched you with his love and given you a place among his people', and they will be asked in a series of post-baptismal questions whether they will live the life of a disciple.

Baptism by full immersion

This has been in use since at least the second century AD and has taken several forms. The individual may be completely submerged by falling backwards into the water or partly submerged and have water poured liberally over the head. It is indeed a moving experience both for the baptized and the onlooker, with powerful symbolism reflecting graphically the dying of the individual to the old life and their being reborn in Christ in the power of the Spirit. A connection may also be made between the water being life-taking, as in drowning, but at the same time life-giving. The idea of washing and cleansing is quite clear here, especially when the newly baptized is clothed in clean white clothes as a sign of purity. Some churches have a purpose-built baptistery but it is possible to use swimming pools and rivers.

The prayers

As mentioned in the previous chapter, it may be possible to personalize one or two prayers in response to any particular anxieties or losses mentioned by members of the baptism families. These can then be included towards the end of the service together with more general prayers (if it is not part of a Communion service) and ending with the Lord's Prayer. At the end of this chapter there is a selection chosen from a variety of sources which you may find helpful.

Choosing music

It is easy to stereotype categories of churchgoers and the music you think they will like. However, the irregular churchgoer may not prefer modern church music whereas some grandparents love to clap along with the noisiest chorus. Experience shows that it is the unchurched who, if they know any hymns at all, know the ones they used to sing at school; and some of the older generation are just as happy with Graham

Kendrick songs and hymns as 'Abide with me'. What is most important is to strike a balance – not simply to keep the peace, but in order to recognize and acknowledge the valid needs and preferences of a variety of people, both those within and without the usual congregation.

It is helpful to know what song books are used by your local schools and to make links with the children's work being done in the parish. Here are some popular compilations:

> *Songs for Every Season*, *Songs for Every Day*, *Songs for Every Easter* and *Songs for Every Christmas*, all produced by Out of the Ark Music and written by Mark and Helen Johnson; available from The School House, 15 Esher Green, Esher, Surrey KT10 8AA.
>
> *Come and Praise*, BBC Books, compiled by Geoffrey Marshall-Taylor, 1990.
>
> *Jump Up if You're Wearing Red*, National Society/Church House Publishing, 1996.

Thanksgiving for the Birth of a Child

Some parents feel that they cannot make the promises required in a baptism service, or are reluctant to pursue baptism for some other reason, and yet want to mark the occasion of birth and their deep sense of thanksgiving for their new infant. Others may be deeply committed Christians but disagree with infant baptism and cannot cope with the concept of promising on behalf of a child, preferring to leave their children to make their own commitment in due course. For these people, the Thanksgiving Service from the ASB provides an opportunity to do just that – give thanks.

The Affirmation of Baptismal Faith

It is not uncommon for some adult Christians to want to make a public declaration of faith, especially if they feel that at the time of their baptism or confirmation they had not fully thought through the issues for themselves. It is not possible to be rebaptized but in the new services there is provision for the affirmation of faith with or without the presence of a bishop. This may happen in the context of a baptism/confirmation/eucharistic service or stand on its own. Those wishing to make such a commitment are called upon to affirm (not replace) their baptismal faith with a new declaration. They say:

I answer the call of God my creator.

I trust in Jesus Christ as my Saviour.

I seek new life from the Holy Spirit.

The congregation responds:

God, who has called you, is faithful.

Rejoice in your baptism into Jesus Christ.

Walk with us in the life of the Spirit.

The Appendices

These should be seen as an integral part of the book, to be digested and used, rather than simply optional reading.

Appendix 1 simply provides a prayer to be said in thanksgiving for the birth of the children who are to be baptized during the service (which should not be confused with the Thanksgiving Service). It may be used at the very beginning of the service as part of the greeting.

Appendix 2 gives some seasonal material under the following headings: Epiphany/Baptism of Christ/Trinity; Easter/Pentecost; All Saints. These are designed as supplements to the main text in the same way that books such as *Lent, Holy Week and Easter* and *Promise of His Glory* have provided such alternatives. The material relates to the baptism service *per se* but also to baptism within a eucharistic context. Each section contains special introductions, collects, baptismal prayers, words at the peace, prayers of intercession, post-communion prayer and blessing.

The notes in the service book state that from the First Sunday of Advent to the Feast of the Presentation and from the First Sunday of Lent to Trinity Sunday the normal lectionary collect and readings should be used. However, the alternative collects and readings provided should be used when baptism is the predominant part of the service. Ministers will need to consider the break in continuity of readings if they are following the new lectionary.

Appendices 3 and 4 replace the standard prayer over the water and the prayers of intercession with responsive forms; some are provided for each season. Where appropriate, they may be sung. These are helpful in providing not only apt material for liturgical seasons but also variety for congregations that have many baptisms, and they underline the role of the congregation in the worship.

Appendix 5 is a table of Bible readings and psalms, divided into seasonal sections and including Old Testament and New Testament lessons. These are not the same as the revised common lectionary and may affect the continuity of the readings from one Sunday to another. Clear directions are given about which readings take precedence and these guidelines need to be observed.

Appendix 6 provides a Litany of the Resurrection for use in procession to the font; it may be said or sung.

Appendix 7 is a simpler threefold profession of faith in the form of a shorter and responsive credal statement; the response 'I believe and trust in him' will be very familiar, but the words said by the president have been changed.

It is apparent that the new baptismal liturgy holds within it all the former strands of theology and practice and will be easily recognizable and feel familiar to all who have been using the ASB service; but the new initiation rites provide a whole package of services which have more substance and content to them than before. They give opportunities for a far richer worship which demonstrates in word, action and symbol the vital nature of initiation into the Church. They should be used with confidence and delight.

Prayers[7]
FOR THE CHURCH

> *Heavenly Father,*
> *we thank you that we belong*
> *to your Church throughout the world,*
> *crossing boundaries of time and space.*
> *We pray for our brothers and sisters in every place,*
> *those who have gone before us,*
> *those who will come after us,*

and those who walk with us now.

Keep us loyal to you and to one another,

faithful to our promises,

and mindful of our unity

for Jesus Christ's sake. Amen.

Lord God,

we pray for the members of this congregation

and all who worship at St...............

Give them childlike hearts

and simple trust.

When they fail, forgive them,

when they fall, uplift them,

and give them grace to learn

from the children in their midst. Amen.

FOR PARENTS

God our heavenly Father,

we thank you for the gift of parenthood

and for the gift of this child, so precious in your sight;

we thank you for those who care for mothers and babies in hospital or at home.

Grant that N and N may always remember your love for them

and seek your guidance in their work as parents,

knowing that you are the one, perfect, heavenly Father. Amen.

Direct with loving kindness these parents, O God;

When they are tired, strengthen them;

when they are worried, sustain them;

when they are bewildered, encourage them;

and in all their fears give them your hope and peace,

  that their lives may be renewed
  today, tomorrow and for ever. Amen.[8]

  Heavenly Father,
  we are not perfect parents,
  our homes are not perfect homes.
  So bless us and our families,
  be with us as we make mistakes,
  guide us as we struggle,
  and help us to listen and learn
  from you, the perfect, holy Father. Amen.

FOR GODPARENTS

  Bless, we pray, those who have made promises today,
  that they may be given wisdom and strength
  to live as Christian witnesses.
  Keep them faithful, loyal and true
  and make them lights in the
  lives of their godchildren. Amen.

FOR THE CHILD

  Lord God,
  this child begins a new journey today.
  Be with him *as* he *steps out in faith,*
  be within him *as* he *seeks to do your will,*
  be before and behind him *as* he *makes* his *way*
  on the Christian pilgrimage. Amen.

FOR FRIENDS AND FAMILY WHO HAVE DIED

Lord God,

in baptism, we die with you and rise again to new life.

We pray for those whom we have loved but see no more;

we thank you that we are united with them through your death and resurrection,

and wait, with hope, for your promises of new life,

through Jesus Christ our Lord. Amen.

GENERAL

O Lord our God,

grant us grace to desire thee with our whole heart,

so that, desiring thee,

we may seek and find thee;

and loving thee may hate those sins

which separate us from thee,

for the sake of Jesus Christ. Amen. [9]

O gracious and holy Father,

give us wisdom to perceive thee,

diligence to seek thee,

patience to wait for thee,

eyes to behold thee,

a heart to meditate upon thee,

and a life to proclaim thee;

through the power of the spirit of Jesus Christ our Lord. Amen. [10]

TALKS AND RESOURCES FOR BAPTISM SERVICES

The practicalities of the service and the building

The practicalities and logistics of conducting baptism services are as important as a right understanding of the liturgy and these can be a great help or hindrance to the congregation.

THE FONT

The placing of the font is of vital importance and two main issues have to be considered. The first relates to the theology of baptism and what initiation is all about, both now and in the past; the second to the size of the congregation and whether the baptism must be visible to them.

History and tradition place some restrictions on the conduct of the service because the font stood originally in a separate baptistery or by the main entrance with restricted space and visibility. In the early Church, baptism took place in a separate room of the church to underline the fact that it was the first stage of a journey, a true initiation rite, after which the baptized entered the church proper. Similarly, the font by the door symbolizes the locus of entry both to the church building and the church body. If you practise full immersion, then the 'font' is in a fixed position.

While we understand the significance of positioning the font by the door, this does pose several problems. If there is only one baptism in an afternoon service with a few friends and family present, then it may be easy enough to accommodate them all at the back of the church; but now that there is a marked preference for incorporating baptisms into the main service, practical difficulties arise. Every church family must consider all the options and make its own decision about how baptism will be conducted. So what are the possibilities?

- Many churches have a second, mobile font which they can position centrally in front of or in place of the nave altar. The disadvantage is that these tend to be smaller and less attractive; there is still something deeply comforting about a solid, stone font and the idea of a font as a thing of convenience to be wheeled in and out at will may lead to a denigration of its importance. The outweighing advantage is that it can be moved into position as and when required and just as easily moved away again afterwards.

  If the only other font is in a secluded baptistery then perhaps there is no sensible alternative. Further information on this can be found in *Repitching the Tent* by Richard Giles.[1]

- If your font is by the main door and at the back of the church, you may choose to conduct the major part of the service from the front of the church, only moving to the font with the family just before the prayer over the water. The rest of the congregation can be asked to turn round to see as much as they can in an effort to underline the theology of community involvement.

SEATING THE FAMILY

As we have seen, where the family sits depends on where the font is; if it is at the back, then this is where families might prefer to be so that they can see everything. Particular consideration should be given to where the family is invited to sit if the baptism occurs during another main service, especially a Communion service. With the best of polite intentions, visiting families are often given what are perceived to be the 'best' seats in the house, right in the front. This is fine if they are familiar and comfortable with your church (or indeed, any church) services, but if they are not, to make them more relaxed, it is better for them to be three or four rows back so that they have the security of regular members of the congregation in front of them. They can then see when to stand, sit or kneel, because there is nothing more embarrassing for the unconfident than having to look over their shoulder to decide what they should be doing. Even if clear directions are given by word or in print, they will feel more secure.

69

'KEEPING THE CHILDREN AMUSED'

By their very nature, baptism service congregations include a number of small children. In a straight baptism service there should be enough activity to keep them interested because the baptismal liturgy, perhaps more than any other, has a great deal of symbolism and action. However, if the baptism is part of a longer celebration you may like to provide some suitable diversionary activities beyond the normal crèche facilities. This is not to mollify any members of the congregation who dislike children, but to make life easier for visiting families. One way of trying to keep both parties happy is to provide quiet activities for children to do either in their pews or in some other part of the church where they can be occupied without feeling excluded. Most enlightened churches have such areas already (see Chapter 8 for more ideas).

COMING UP FOR A BLESSING

Bringing children for baptism can often be the beginning of a new faith or the rekindling of a dying faith for parents and other adults. They may be unfamiliar with Communion services and wonder whether or not to take communion. A simple announcement to the effect that everybody is welcome to come up for a blessing or to receive communion if they are communicant in their own churches will be helpful. Similarly, it also needs to be said that it is quite acceptable *not* to come up to the altar rail.

INVOLVING THE CONGREGATION

Services with many visitors should be seen as evangelistic opportunities, not simply in the sense of preaching the gospel message or receiving the sacrament. Visitors will judge the Church (and therefore God) by the welcome they receive and the attitude of regulars to them and their children. Evangelism and behaviour are very closely linked. The congregation needs reminding that it is their task as the people of God to approach strangers with a smile, offer them coffee, give them newcomers' welcome packs and generally make them feel that church is a comfortable place to be and a place to which they might return. There is something quite hypocritical about a congregation which proclaims the words of welcome one moment only to be glaring at noisy three-year-olds the next, implying by facial expression if not by actual words that it would be better for everybody if the child were removed to a distant room. On the other hand, one can sympathize with long-suffering congregations when they have to tolerate a disturbance level which is unreasonable. Keeping the balance requires the wisdom of Solomon and needs careful and constant consideration.

While it might show a lack of dedication, commitment or stickability on their part, newcomers will give churches very few chances to prove themselves. It will not (generally) be matters of theology or doctrine which prevent them exploring faith further but the fact that nobody spoke to them, somebody glared at them or they felt uncomfortable and excluded. Don't miss or mess up an opportunity: this message needs to be heard loud and clear by congregations at periodic intervals. It may be necessary to practise and explain the congregational responses from time to time, to preach on their role, to write magazine or newsletter articles and to talk about individual and corporate responsibilities in baptism matters. Appendix 3 of the service book has many good responsive prayers which will involve the congregation even more fully, and in the 'Welcome' they have a crucial role to play.

Preaching at baptisms

There is a wealth of material available for planning sermons and addresses appropriate to acts of worship involving children. Perhaps the key word to bear in mind is that they should be *appropriate* – appropriate to the circumstances and context of the service and congregation. As we have seen, baptisms occur at a variety of times, but with those families who are not regular members of the church or who are relative newcomers, this may be a rare opportunity to have a meaningful impact and leave them wanting to know more about the Christian faith.

BAPTISMS AT THE MAIN SERVICE

If your church has a monthly Eucharist with baptisms, you may not want to have a sermon specifically about baptism every time, as this is rather limiting. Any Christian message should be relevant to baptism families because it will be about some aspect of faith and, in any event, it is possible to refer to baptism, if only in passing, whatever the theme for the day. Parents do not expect the whole service to be built around them but are delighted if there is a personal touch in mentioning the child's name during the talk and they can see that there is a sense of cohesion to the whole service.

BAPTISM AT A SERVICE OF THE WORD

If the service is primarily a baptism service and the whole congregation has come for that reason, then it is reasonable to expect a baptismal address. But there are certain key points which need to be borne in mind.

- Baptism congregations will include a number of children of all ages, as well as adults who will be a mixture of committed Christians and uninterested friends and relatives. This means that the talk must not patronize the children or ignore the adults.

- It is possible to speak to a gathering of all ages without excluding the five-year-old or the 95-year-old and addresses should not be aimed at one group to the detriment of others. It is true that we can never please everybody all the time but there should be something to which people of all ages can relate. Most of the major baptismal themes can be introduced in a way with which young children can identify (especially since there are so many visible symbols) but which can be developed so that they evoke responses in adults.

- Children do not have to understand everything, any more than adults and provided that enough is accessible they will learn as much from the experience and atmosphere as from the 'teaching'. As with all worship, the heart as well as the head needs to be involved, the feelings as well as the thoughts.

- The talk should err on the side of brevity. This is not the service for a lengthy exposition of Romans 6 or a detailed analysis of sacramental theology, however learned and enlightening. Parents will be concerned with keeping the baby quiet, willing older siblings not to ask to go to the loo in a loud voice and wondering how to cope with long-running family feuds which threaten to erupt over the sausage rolls. A short, well-constructed, well-delivered talk is what is needed.

- Visual aids are often helpful, but they must be exactly that — visual and aids. Don't produce objects or pictures which can only be seen by the front row; and don't use anything which does not aid the purpose of the talk, however fascinating or interesting it may be. The symbols of the liturgy provide excellent visual aids in their own right and require no extra preparation time, so use them as much as you can.

- The ability of small children to listen, sit still and behave varies enormously from one family to another. Children must be in attendance at such services, but there is a balance between making families feel at home on the one hand and allowing children to use the church as an adventure playground on the other.

KNOW YOUR CHILDREN

If you are a parent or teacher, you will have some understanding of the way children tick. If not, observe them as you work with them and learn from your mistakes. If you feel totally out of your depth, then find others in the congregation to give the talks or advise you. Here are some useful things to know:

- Children may not give the answer you are looking for, however obvious it seems to you; e.g. in a misguided attempt to talk about repentance to junior school children, a comparison was made between washing our faces in the morning with making clean what's inside us. 'How might we do that?' was the innocent question. Back came the reply: 'Eat lots of fruit.'

- Some children are simply perverse and will purposely give you the wrong answer or an embarrassing answer in order to test your reaction. Some seven-year-olds *do* know what the seventh commandment is and love to let you know.

- Infants think *literally* and see things in concrete terms: 'a blanket of snow' or 'a carpet of flowers' will have them wondering who left the blanket or the carpet outside.

- Children do not compartmentalize life, so the past and the present are often confused. They remember half a story and are adept at finding the other half from elsewhere. Thus, they might say that we eat pancakes during Lent because Jesus cooked some for the devil on some stones in the wilderness.

- Children are honest and say what they think: 'I'm not praying for him because I don't like him.'

- Children flourish on encouragement, so be careful how you tell a child that their answer is wrong. Say: 'That's an interesting answer but I wonder if anybody has any other ideas,' or 'I hadn't thought of that,' or even 'I don't think that's quite right.'

- There are ways of getting children to sit quietly for a few minutes while the talk or the prayers are going on. They can sit round the Paschal candle and watch it in case it goes out while the minister says the final prayers, or you might ask them to count quietly all the crosses they can see in the church while you talk about the meaning of the cross, or all the stained-glass windows or candles while you talk about the light of Christ.

- The 'here's one I made earlier' principle is helpful – a selection of pre-prepared pictures for the youngest to colour in with the chance to show off their handiwork at the end – but this approach becomes tedious if over-used and should not be seen as an alternative to carefully prepared visual aids. But you may feel that these are merely distractions to the real work of the service and that your talk should be able to incorporate the needs of all ages and have something for everybody. We agree and quite often we manage it, but it's always useful to have some external aids up your sleeve.

The all-age talk

We have noted already that all-age talks do not have to be patronizing or lengthy. Simple does not mean trite; meaningful does not mean erudite. They will be theological if they speak of God and draw the listeners closer to God in one way or another and this can be done simply but effectively.

There are many good resource books but here are some outline notes which can be expanded. The new liturgy gives suggested readings and psalms for special seasons and you will need to prepare your talk in line with those. In each case we provide a title, a theme, visual aids, suggestions for content and, where appropriate, questions that could be asked, as well as a conclusion and Bible references.

1 JOURNEY/PILGRIMAGE

Theme: The Christian life is a long process; baptism is the beginning of the journey. You may choose to focus on the child to be baptized while reminding the congregation that the journey is theirs as well.

Visual aids: Things needed on a journey – map, compass, train ticket, lunch box, rucksack/suitcase, anorak.

Content/Questions: Becoming a Christian involves a journey. Refer to somebody who went on a journey. Paddington Bear came all the way from Peru with marmalade sandwiches under his hat (when using popular characters from TV and books, make sure that they really are popular and not relics of your own childhood).

Ask what things you would take on that kind of journey.

Talk about the things the child will need on his or her Christian journey: Bible, prayer books, Christian friends and godparents (to help when they get lost). You could mention signposts and the everyday reminders that they are not travelling alone: other baptisms, confirmation services, school assemblies, people asking to be married in church, people who mention the importance of God or Jesus Christ in their lives, people who pray, the church building and the people who gather there.

Conclusion: This child has started on a Christian journey. God promises to be their constant companion, knowing the best route, knowing what they'll find easy and what will be hard work. He offers other people to walk with them and help them. In the process they will grow in wisdom and love.

Bible passage: Luke 24.13-31.

2 PROMISES

Theme: We are all making promises today which we will try to keep; God makes promises to us that he always keeps.

Visual aids: A Cub/Brownie membership card; a rainbow on a large sheet of card.

Content/Questions: What does a promise mean? Can anybody think of a promise they made which was hard to keep? Talk about the Brownie/Cub Scout promise if old enough children are present. In baptism, parents and godparents make promises – what are they? They mean to keep them and they set out with good intentions but it's not easy – who will help them?

What does God's Church promise? It promises to be there for everyone. It is the place where we can come with others and ask God for forgiveness when we fail to keep our promises. It is the place where we are reminded of the promises we have made and encouraged to do better. It promises to be a support and to provide the place where we can worship together. When spoken in church, the baptism promises are a reminder to all Christians of the promises they have made and must try to keep.

What does God promise to do? He promises to love you without limit; to guide you; to be close to you when life is very hard. He promises to forgive you when you fail. The rainbow is the special sign for Christians and Jews that God always keeps his promises (story of Noah).

Conclusion: God never breaks his promise to us – to be there for us and forgive us when we fail. We must try to follow his example and keep the promises we make.

Bible passages: Genesis 9.8-17 and 17.1-8; Exodus 6.2-9.

3 LIGHT AND CANDLES

Theme: Jesus is the light of the world – his light never goes out and will always shine for us. Christians also carry the light of Jesus Christ within them.

Visual aids: Selection of lights and lamps, matches, miner's helmet, reading lamp, torch, roadworks lamp, warning lights, helmet lights, never-ending candles, etc. Baptism candle/Paschal candle.

Content/Questions: What do you use lights for? How many different ones can you think of? Talk about what lights are for: advance warning, protection, seeing in the dark, protecting ships.

Sometimes children and adults are frightened of the dark and seek a light to make them feel safe.

Jesus described himself as a light. He isn't actually a light, but he is a very special person who can do some of the things that lights do. He acts like a warning light (e.g. to stop you being selfish and making bad decisions); he is a constant friend with us when we feel the world is full of darkness, and he helps to remove our fears; he shows us what direction we should go in in life, much as a light reveals the right path for us to walk along.

Conclusion: In baptism you receive a lighted candle, to show that Jesus' light has come into your life. He will always be there. The darkness of our lives will never overcome his special light and as we grow in faith we will shine a light into other people's lives on Jesus' behalf.

Bible passages: John 1.1-14 and 8.12.

4 THE SIGN OF THE CROSS

Theme: In baptism we are indelibly marked with an invisible cross as a sign of identity.

Visual aids: Selection of badges – blazer, swimming, cubs, monitor, blue team, RAF, medals, football shirt.

Content/Questions: What are badges for? How do you know which football team your friend supports?

Badges tell us about the person, what they are like, what they do. You can see them everywhere. You have to do something to be allowed to wear the badge, e.g. be eight to be a cub, be chosen for the team. You are expected to behave well – and not to let down the reputation of your club/organization.

Baptism is like a badge which can't be rubbed out or taken away. It's invisible but we know it's there. Anybody who wants to can become a member of this family and wear the badge but those who wear it will be expected to try to behave like Jesus did; and if they fail, to say sorry.

You could also talk about the way some junior football players want to wear replica shirts of favourite league 'stars', and that this can inspire them to greater efforts. The sign of the cross can similarly inspire, especially when we remember that the 'powerful' Holy Spirit comes and dwells within the life of the newly baptized. In either case, we have to work hard to live up to the identity we have chosen for ourselves.

Conclusion: Remember with pride the moment when your child was signed with the cross of Christ. Recall the moment of your own baptism and ask God to inspire you to live up to your identity as a Christian.

Bible passage: Mark 8.34-38.

5 DEATH AND RESURRECTION

Theme: Baptism is about dying with Christ in order to be raised to new life – both now and in eternity.

Visual aids: Seeds/bulbs/vegetables that grow underground.

Content/Questions: Talk about bulbs having to be in the dark before they bloom. Ask in which season of the year the ground is bare and lifeless and when plants and trees come to life. Although God created the world and loves it very much, there are things about us which sadden him and which he wants us to change. These things are so important that we say we must put to death the things that are wrong in our lives so that we can live new lives as God would wish. In baptism we link the idea of our putting to death what is wrong in us in order to live a good new life, with the reality of Jesus' life and death. He allowed himself to be put to death and, in the process, took with him all the world's wrongs. When he was brought to new life by God through his resurrection, he gave us all the power to put sin behind us and to live a new life where good reigns. Sometimes, choosing to do the right thing can feel like a death, especially when we put others first rather than giving in to our own powerful, selfish or greedy desires.

Conclusion: As baptized Christians we must accept the feelings of loss and death associated with resisting the impulse to greed, selfishness and self-comfort at the expense of others; but as we do this new things come to life in us. Joy in the happiness that our actions may have brought others; a sense of peace and being in harmony with the creation and ourselves; the realization that what we thought were our deepest needs turned out not to be; and acknowledging that we have a deeper purpose that we had not appreciated.

Bible passages: Romans 6.1-11; John 20.1-10.

6 BIRTHDAYS AND FAMILIES

Theme: Baptism is like having another kind of birthday but with an extended family.

Visual aids: Balloons, a cake, a present. Letter from a vicar introducing a Christian who has moved to a new parish or country.

Content/Questions: Why do we have a birthday? Anybody with a birthday today, this week, this month, the same day as mine?

Baptism is like having a different kind of birthday. When a baby is born they become a member of their own family – Watson, Smith, etc. When they are baptized they become a member of the worldwide Church and belong to a huge family.

You might talk about/ask questions about the similarities between birthdays and baptisms. Family party/cakes/presents; and then go on to remind people that in the baptism celebration extra people are taking part, i.e. members of that new worldwide family.

When you become a member of the family you are welcomed and accepted wherever you go. If you have an uncle in Australia then he might invite you to visit. In the same way, if you travel as a Christian you should receive a welcome in every church you visit. You could talk about your own experiences of meeting new Christians or of having visitors from other countries to your own church. The baptism party itself may include Christians from other congregations and you could ask them how it feels coming to your church and meeting other members of their Christian family.

On another occasion you might vary the theme slightly to concentrate on the distinctive features of family members – hair colour, outlook on life; and then explore the distinctive features of the Christian family. Although the members are not perfect, you should see a desire to worship God, to grow in faith and understanding and to serve others for the sake of God rather than for any other reward. It is up to you to live so that others see the likeness between you and Jesus.

Conclusion: (N) has become a Christian. Wherever he or she goes, to any village or city in the world, they can expect to be welcomed by fellow Christians and share a common inheritance/common values. Encourage him or her in the membership of this new family, and give them every opportunity to get to know other members and to acquire the distinctive features of a member of the Christian family.

Bible passages: Ephesians 2.19; Matthew 28.16-20.

7 THE BEST GIFT

Theme: Jesus and the Holy Spirit are the most precious gifts we can receive.

Visual aids: Presents, expensive items and homemade ones, wrapping paper.

Content/Questions: What is the best present you've ever had? What would you like most of all?

Talk about presents – how do you choose them, what was the last present you gave? Who do you give presents to and why?

There are some presents that cost very little, financially, but which are very precious: framed photographs, homemade cards or things that you have crafted yourself. Sometimes the gifts we receive are not physical at all – a loving embrace, a word of wisdom, encouragement and praise. These are gifts that you cannot buy in shops.

Today this child is to receive the most precious gift of all. It is the gift of acceptance by God and the love of his Son Jesus Christ. As they learn more about the gift they have been given, they will discover that it is worth more than gold and precious jewels. They will have a guide and companion through life, someone who will not walk away when they do wrong, someone with great wisdom who will praise and encourage but also challenge them to live their lives in the best way possible.

Conclusion: Things that are expensive do not necessarily cost a lot of money. Valuable things don't always come in expensive-looking boxes. And as each person receives the gift of Jesus Christ they are able to offer similar gifts to others – sharing someone's pain, taking their side against the crowd. Due to their cost these things are not often chosen as gifts, though people would love to receive them. Baptism is about receiving this sort of gift from God and learning to give similar gifts to others.

Bible passages: John 3.16-21 Matthew 2.1-12.

8 THE WATER OF LIFE

Theme: The water of baptism speaks of our value to God and his desire to make us spiritually clean.

Visual aids: Water of baptism. Bottle of muddy water. Baby bath.

Content/Questions: We take clean water for granted most of the time. Droughts of recent years, though, have made us realize that it is a limited resource. Ask if anyone can name countries where clean water is difficult to get. And if anyone has lived in such a place.

Talk about the value of water when Jesus was alive. It had to be carried from wells or from the river. It was a sign of great friendship to offer guests water to wash their feet when they came into your house from the dusty conditions outside.

The water of baptism is very precious. We only have it as a result of Jesus living the life he did and of his being willing to give up his life to show the extent of his love for us. We use it freely today to show Jesus' love and acceptance of this child and his desire that they become his friend and servant for the rest of their lives.

Water is also the way in which we wash ourselves clean. It is very difficult to get clean without water. The water of baptism symbolizes our deep inner cleansing by God in the power of his Holy Spirit. And as this child grows into adulthood, God offers daily to wash away his or her failures, which means that they can bring their failings to God with sorrow but with confidence, knowing of his cleansing forgiveness.

Conclusion: Never take baptism for granted. The water we use here today is very precious. It is a sign of Jesus' love for this child and it is a sign of inner cleansing so that they may always seek forgiveness for their failures and never be separated from his love.

Bible passages: 1 Peter 3.18-22; John 4.7-26; Mark 1.4-11.

9   PEOPLE WHO LOOK AFTER US

Theme: There are special people to look after us.

Visual aids: Things used by nursery school teacher, doctor, etc.; hats belonging to policemen, firemen.

Content/Questions: Who looks after a new-born baby? Who looks after you? Talk about people who help us and look after us at different times of our lives. Talk about the things they do for us.

Ask about the things we do for other people. There may be people in the congregation who have special responsibilities at home or at work. Children may sometimes have to help in the care of younger brothers and sisters.

There are also people who help us learn about God and get to know him. Godparents, parents, clergy, baptism visitors, other members of the congregation or those who run the crèche or youth group. Others undertake training to help us understand the Bible or help to keep the church alive as a place where we can worship God, baptize children and help adults grow in faith and service.

Talk about all the different people who helped to make this service possible, including the cleaners and the flower arrangers and those who paid for the building and its running costs.

Jesus Christ was the most special person who showed us all just how much God loves us and how much he longs for us to love and serve him.

And down through the ages saints and many other people of faith have carried the message so that you might hear and receive it again today. You might see some of them in the stained-glass windows.

Conclusion: Don't take God or those who look after you for granted. There are so many people who look after us: our parents, godparents and grandparents, friends, neighbours and family as well as Christians now and through the ages who point to the God who created us all.

Bible passage: Luke 10.25-37.

10   JESUS IS THE WAY

Theme: Jesus is a reliable guide in your life on earth.

Visual aids: Compass, map, badges of office (e.g. National Trust guide, Girl Guide), tourist board leaflets.

Content/Questions: Who are the people we need to seek guidance from if we are to get through life? How do we find out if they are likely to be reliable? Talk about the importance we place on the recommendations of people we trust and of official organizations that guarantee trustworthiness. Which books do we treat as reliable and which are deceptive? Which characters are made up (e.g. Superman) and which are real? Talk about the fact that as we grow up we realize which people are only imaginary and which are real. When you talk to a group of children, they are usually quite accurate in their assessment of the validity of different characters. In the minds of most people, Jesus Christ is accepted as a historic person. His life as recorded in the gospels is an inspiration and guide for Christians throughout the world. The Bible teaches us that he is loving, that his purposes are always good and that we were made to love and serve him. The Church is made up of people who believe his Spirit lives within them, giving them direction and purpose in their daily lives.

Conclusion: You can be certain that Jesus will guide you through the power of prayer, through the accounts of his life recorded in the Bible and through his followers – Christians who have his Spirit living within them.

Take the opportunity today to ask Jesus to be your daily guide and inspiration. He will not let you down.

Bible passages: John 14.1-6; Luke 24.13-27.

11 THE PARENTHOOD OF GOD

Theme: To understand that God loves us deeply but that he limits his power for our sake.

Visual aids: Pictures of adults holding babies and smiling at them and parents playing with toddlers. Magazine pictures of fast cars and big houses. Whiteboard and pens.

Content/Questions: Talk about the way a relationship of love is formed between a parent and their child. Smiling at a baby draws out an answering smile from them. Cuddle a small child and they will put their arms around your neck in return. Ask what emotions adults and children feel when they are smiled at and cuddled.

Now ask about the ways in which parents, godparents and other significant adults support our growth and the ways in which they can inhibit growth. Look at how too much attention or support is as harmful as too little. Children who do not have to take responsibility for anything and rely on parents for everything, even when they are older, never grow up or become fully adult. Those who are pushed too hard to achieve great things or who have unrealistic expectations placed upon them will buckle under the pressure or may come to think that they will only be loved for what they achieve.

Baptism marks the beginning of another relationship of love and support. God, our heavenly Father, rejoices at our birth and our baptism and has loved us from before birth. Imagine a picture of God holding your child and smiling. When we begin to appreciate his love for us there is a welling up of joy in our hearts.

Now think about what we look for in our relationship with God. Do we ask him to solve all our problems and provide all the answers so that we never think for ourselves? Or can we see that he needs to be careful about the extent and nature of his support for us? He must be careful not to overwhelm us or impede our growth to maturity.

Conclusion: Invite the congregation to think of phrases for a prayer for the newly baptized: phrases which reflect the fact that they must be allowed to experience pains as well as joys in order to build up their own strength of character; phrases which recognize the love God has for them and help them to realize that God wants them to learn to love him for himself rather than for what he can do for them.

Bible passages: Hosea 11.1-4; Luke 15.11-24.

12   FAITH IN THE BALANCE

Theme: Many people hold faith 'in the balance'. Seeing the balance within can link daily experience to further faith development.

Visual aid: Set of scales (double pan variety).

Content/Questions: It is rarely true that anyone is completely indifferent to faith. Our life experience adds to one or other of the pans: for example, a loving and Christian grandparent; a cynical RE teacher; the death of a loved one; a wedding service conducted with care; TV pictures of a mudslide; the editorial slant of our favourite paper. All these affect the way we think and feel about matters of faith.

Invite the congregation to recognize the scales of faith within themselves. Ask them to think back over their past and recall the things that have given them faith in God, and those things which have challenged it. Suggest that they think now about what this service of baptism means to them, and the building in which it is taking place. You could mention the notice boards as evidence of human activity built around a faith in God and his love for the world; or the sacrifice of finance and time that contributed towards the building and its upkeep. Parents and godparents have accepted responsibility to encourage their child in the Christian faith. They will only be able to do this to the extent that they themselves feel that faith weighs heavily in their lives. But they are not alone. The community of faith, the Church, is there to support and encourage them. God knows how weak we are alone and calls us to share our faith with one another. Encourage them to see this baptism as something positive to weigh in the balance.

Conclusion: Acknowledge the faith you have and determine to consider this more often in your life. Recognize that modern life witnesses only rarely to the importance of faith in life. In this present age it can be deeply unfashionable to be a Christian. See this baptism as an important moment of faith, not only in the life of the child but in all your lives. Finally, don't be too hard on yourself. You may have more faith than you give yourself credit for.

Bible passages: Hebrews 11.32-39; Mark 9.14-29.

It is often possible to choose a theme which fits in with the church calendar, however loosely. Thus, 'The best gift' is particularly suitable at Christmas or Epiphany, 'Light and candles' at Advent or Christmas, 'The sign of the cross' at Passiontide or Easter – whereas others, such as 'Birthdays and families', are more general. The particular nature of the congregation of the day needs to be borne in mind, too, so that the most appropriate talk is chosen for that occasion.

Section Four

Baptism:
Follow-up

8

AFTER BAPTISM –
WHAT NEXT?

The baptismal liturgy gives much attention to the wider church family and the responsibilities of the local congregation to join in the pilgrimage of faith (see Chapter 7). It is easy for the Church to pay lip-service to the words of the liturgy month by month without taking them to heart; easy to agree in theory with the theology while neglecting the on-going practical implications.

It is incumbent upon churches to ensure that the baptism service is the beginning and not the end of a beautiful and meaningful relationship, and there are many opportunities for building on the work which has already been done. Many things might happen in the ideal church, but inevitably a perfect blueprint will not always be achievable. Most churches, however, will want to consider carefully what they can provide and do as much as they can to the best of their ability.

After the baptism

- Babies who were baptized at a service which did not include the regular congregation can be welcomed at the next Sunday morning service. Just before the Peace (in a Communion service), parents can be invited to come with their infants to the front of the church to be welcomed by name. Prior to the welcome, ministers may wish to use the congregational questions and responses from the baptism service to reinforce the importance of their role. Some churches use this opportunity to give the certificate and baptismal candle – a sure way of encouraging families to come.

- Within four weeks of the service, baptism visitors can deliver the certificate by hand (if it has not been given in the service), preferably when both parents are at home. They might take the parish magazine, Toddler Club Newsletter or other relevant publications. This may turn out to be little more than a doorstep encounter, but it may develop into a real conversation and even regular members of the congregation will feel that they have been given some special attention. In any event, contact has been renewed, information imparted and parents are reminded once again that the church is alive and well.

- Details of baptism families can be given to leaders of relevant church groups such as a Toddler Club, so that they can be invited to future events.

- This is a good time to include other members of the family, too, so if there are older siblings who might be eligible for Sunday School, Pathfinders, etc., make sure that they receive invitations to join in.

- On the first, second and third anniversaries, baptism visitors could post or deliver anniversary cards but the efficacy of these is variable and depends upon the degree of mobility of families within your area. If it is a stable community where families are likely to be living in the same house two or three years on, then such cards can be a great asset and a good reminder to parents that the local church still wants to communicate with them. Messages or invitations can be inserted where appropriate.

Cards can be bought in bulk from the Mothers' Union or SPCK, but you need to choose which is most appropriate for your locality. Some of them provide an adult message for parents and are quite wordy while others are more suitable for the child. Even better would be to make your own, using desktop publishing, so that you can personalize them according to your own preferences. This is the kind of job which can be done well in advance by somebody with word-processing skills.

However, there are some pitfalls. If the population is mobile, baptism visitors can find themselves continually arriving on the doorstep only to find that the family has moved on; this can be a bad use of time and personnel which could be better employed. Also, some parents express surprise that the church continues to remind them of baptism when they have moved on both mentally and physically and are involved in the next stage of Sunday School or Family Services.

- If your church has special sponsors for children, they should be reminded to look out for 'their' families and take an interest in them.

Annual Thanksgiving for Baptism service

Many churches hold an annual Thanksgiving for Baptism service to which all the families who have had children baptized within the previous three years are invited. This provides a reminder of the church's presence and strengthens or renews links until the child is old enough to come to Sunday School (or the equivalent). Inevitably, some families have moved away but an encouraging number still turn up. This is an ideal opportunity for the congregation to fulfil the promises they have made in the service: to welcome, uphold and support the newly baptized. They can do this by their presence, by being available to hold the baby, sitting with families and introducing people to one another. They know where to go for the picnic; but they might also take part in the preparation and delivery of the service so that it is seen not simply as an act of worship for a specialist group but one that involves the whole people of God, who have specific responsibilities for the nurture of children and young people.

If your church conducts relatively few baptisms, you might hold this service every other year.

There are some general guidelines for planning these services but local context will affect the details. For example, if your parish serves a self-contained village in which nearly all the congregation lives, publicity is easier than in an eclectic church; some communities do not work with diaries and advanced planning and publicity will be last-minute. You must decide for yourself with your own team what will work best.

However, the practical factors are important:

- *Timing:* Sunday afternoon (but not too early or too late!) seems to be a good time, though we know other churches where people prefer Saturday afternoons.

- The *social element* is important, so have a bring-your-own picnic in the vicarage garden, afternoon tea in the hall or whatever your families will respond to. This means that members of the congregation can mingle with the families and get to know one another better.

- *Publicity* is also important and personal letters of invitation, inviting the family with godparents, need to go out early. The service should be advertised in the magazine, at Toddler Club, etc.

- Sponsors or *baptism visitors* should be present, together with other members of the congregation, so that they can welcome and talk to people as they arrive.

- The service needs to be *short*, no more than 30 or 40 minutes, to take account of the many small children present; but it needs to have some adult content, too.

- The *address* needs *visual aids* and must include the older children.

- *Music* should be carefully chosen so that the songs and hymns meet the needs of adults and children alike. Modern music is not always the most well known and you should include some of the favourite songs sung at the toddler or family service, if you have one.

Here is one suggested order of service:

Welcome, invitation to worship and lighting of Paschal candle

Hymn

Prayers, including some simple responsorial prayers about family life, a prayer for parents and godparents and the Lord's Prayer

Children's songs (as sung at a weekly toddler service)

Reading or story

Talk

Hymn

Thanksgiving for baptism

Confession and renewal of vows

Hymn

Blessing

This programme caters for the needs of small children but also provides something for the adults. It resonates well with other worship and activities going on in the church and involves many members of the congregation. If numbers are small, it can take place in a side chapel or informal setting outdoors.

Midweek worship for pre-schoolers (called variously toddler services, pram services, under-fives, etc.)

The name of this service is more important than you might think because it provides a sense of identity and purpose and should be more imaginative than 'pram service' (hardly anybody uses prams nowadays). Be careful not to stereotype; *mother* and toddler service is politically incorrect and may be off-putting for fathers and nannies. In our own churches, the groups are called 'Young Vines' and 'First Steppers'.

This is an invaluable way of reaching young families and initiating them into an understanding of belonging to the Christian family. Our groups have had fathers, grannies, childminders, nannies and other significant adults bringing their charges.

Why have special services?

Even parents who are committed to Sunday worship find Sunday mornings difficult for all kinds of practical and social reasons and are delighted to have something geared towards their children. Others may feel that half an hour midweek is all they can manage, especially where one parent is resistant to Christian affiliation. This may not fulfil your vision of totally committed Christians but we have to meet people where they are if we are to build bridges and encourage them to grow in faith. Sunday is often the only free day for family activities and in separated families it may be the day children see the other parent; it is also a prime sports day and, increasingly, a popular time for a shopping expedition.

And even without these inviting distractions, the unchurched or those on the fringes find walking into a full church with children in tow a great ordeal, a fact which is often underestimated by clergy. Even the keenest churchgoer can find life difficult when children come along, so being able to come during the week when the worshippers will have a lot in common feels safer and more inviting. Of course, congregations need to be educated and reminded of the responsibility laid upon them at the baptismal service, so that parents who come on Sundays feel that they are welcomed rather than tolerated.

Parenthood, especially first time round, can be a shock to the system and it is helpful to have a supportive group of like-minded parents plus a number of understanding leaders and helpers who can listen, hold the baby, share fears and joys and be extra friends. On countless occasions, we have witnessed positive exchanges between adult members of the church and toddlers who become surrogate grandchildren, nieces or nephews. It is on these good feelings that the future of that child's Christian life may depend and this is why the response of Christian congregations to youngsters is so important.

In addition to good feelings, the youngest of children can develop a sense of mystery and awe. They will stand still to watch candles and listen to prayers and can enjoy being in a holy place; so we make no apology for building up midweek worship, though we continue to hope and strive towards a deeper Sunday commitment where families can meet with the wider body of the church. It is important to ensure that midweek worship is not seen as second best or anything but 'real' worship. After all, the sabbath was not always a Sunday.

When planning the structure of such services, it is important to remember that familiarity is crucial for small children. Worship leaders may like to have variety and try out new things to keep the attention of the congregation, but children thrive on familiarity – borne out by the desire to have the same story read night after night.

They need to feel secure and know what is happening, so it is good to have patterns which are followed every time, with the variety and distinctiveness coming in the content of the story and activity.

Our **First Steppers Service** always follows this pattern:

A short prayer:

> Lord Jesus, we have come today
>
> to pray to you,
>
> to listen to you,
>
> and to sing to you.
>
> Help us to worship you in our own way. Amen.

Thought for the Day — a two-minute topical and impromptu slot for the adults.

Songs — chosen from a selection of about twenty.

Musical instruments — which always accompany the same song, 'Praise him, praise him all his little children' (instruments are homemade or brought from educational suppliers).

Lighting (and blowing out) *the birthday candle* — which has now become an anniversary, baptism, welcoming newcomers, leavers' candle and includes the adults, absent grannies and the clergy as well as the children.

Story and activity — leaving the child with something to take home (there are countless good books giving ideas but keep it short and simple).

More songs

A final prayer:

> Jesus, friend of little children,
>
> Be a friend to me;
>
> Take my hand and ever keep me
>
> Close to thee.

Notices

Drinks and chat.

The service itself lasts about 25 minutes, the coffee time about 45 minutes and it is here that we do much pastoral and evangelistic work. Newcomers to church are surprised to find that even clergy can pick up crying children and understand what it's like to be frustrated, angry and exhausted as well as joyful, and it's a good opportunity to talk about baptism, confirmation and other church activities.

Parental views

Here are two short accounts from parents about the toddler services they attend:

> *I was baptized and confirmed just over a year before my first child was born. When he arrived there were things I, as a Christian, knew I should do for him – pray for him, have him baptized and teach him about Jesus. The first two were relatively straightforward but the last one was more difficult. Having had no Christian teaching as a child, I did not know the best way to approach this. My answer came in the form of First Steppers, a short weekly service for pre-school children. From just a few weeks old, Daniel and I joined in the songs, prayers and stories. There was no need to worry about him crying or shouting or even running around as he grew older, and he was able to get used to being in church in a relaxed and informal atmosphere. Our involvement in the church has grown over time and we have acquired an extended family of people who really care for others. This was particularly valuable when I had to spend a week in hospital with my eight-month-old daughter. Although we attend Sunday services regularly, the simple messages and stories we hear at First Steppers play a particularly important part in our worship, not just for my children but for me as well. As Jesus said, 'Whoever does not accept the kingdom of God like a child will never enter it.'[1]*

> *Although I want to go to church, my husband is not very keen and anyway Sunday is the only day we always have together. When we had our baby baptized, it was a bit of an issue for us. Going to*

the toddler service every other week with Jessica has made all the difference. I feel relaxed, she enjoys the company of other children and the activity, and my husband is very happy to look at what she has made and hear the story secondhand. Maybe one day we will all go to church together but for now it's a real answer to prayer.[2]

Faith development in the under-fives

You may agree that adults will appreciate such a service but wonder whether pre-school children are too young to worship or understand what is going on. After all, most of them can barely walk or talk, so what use is it to devise an act of worship with a structure, however informal? Would it not be better to stick to the old adage that children should be seen and not heard – at least until they have become civilized human beings?

Research in this field, which is backed up by our experience, suggests that even the youngest infant benefits from belonging to a church. In his works on faith development, John Westerhoff[3] identifies four major styles of faith. He uses the analogy of a tree which, when it is cut down, displays a series of concentric circles which mark the age of the tree. The growth in the early years, he says, is not abandoned but remains at the centre of the tree.

The centre of Westerhoff's tree and the first style is *experienced faith* – a sense of loving acceptance and belonging which the child receives from the church in the same way that he or she receives it from the family. It is the quality of Christian relationships which counts here and without this firm foundation it is difficult to mature as a Christian (or, indeed, as a person). This is not the exclusive province of infants, however; adults need experienced faith, too, and parents who have not had this opportunity as a child will also benefit from being at the midweek service.

Like the tree, faith also grows and where there are appropriate conditions people are enabled to move on to the next style of faith. It is Westerhoff's belief that this growth takes place only within a believing community and that living within the faith community, rather than religious instruction, is the real key to faith development. Belonging to a toddler service is vital; the nature of the stories told or instruction given is of secondary importance, though adults and children enjoy the stories and learn from the activities.

But don't underestimate what children are thinking and picking up. Very quickly, they anticipate what is coming next, learn the actions to songs and know when to say Amen. They seem to learn most quickly what 'Drinks and biscuits time' means!

In church on Sundays

Many families will not graduate to Sunday worship, but some will, especially if there is an accessible service where they feel welcome. There are some things which the congregation can provide to make this transition easier:

- Most importantly, *a genuine welcome* from sidespersons, wardens, clergy and congregation alike. A smiling face will go a long way to keeping people coming to church.

- *Happy bags/pew bags* – simple drawstring bags (hanging on hooks so that they are easily visible) made from bright material (250 x 200 cm is about right) and containing puzzles, notebooks, soft toys, books, crayons, etc. These are always a huge success and will keep even the youngest children quiet as they take out and put back every item several times with a dedication possible only in a two-year-old. There needs to be a 'monitor' who takes responsibility for checking, washing and restocking them periodically. The Mothers' Union are often particularly good at this. An alternative container is a cardboard shoebox covered in bright paper.

- *Boxes or shelves of books for 0–fives*, covered in sticky-back plastic, with somebody responsible for updating them and removing those with chewed-up corners. Books which look as though they have come straight from the Ark should be taken away and replaced. Sometimes baptism families ask if they can make a donation to the church and buying books for children is a popular way of utilizing their generosity.

- Single *pages of simple line drawings* to colour in and a supply of crayons and pencils, but probably *not* felt tips unless you are very brave or not worried about carpets, etc. These can be of biblical characters, candles, a baby, a cross, the church, a stained-glass window, groups of people or whatever your resident artist can draw. Some parishes have an artistic soul who will be delighted to provide originals for photocopying but supplies need checking frequently and half-coloured, half-eaten pictures removed.

- All these items need to be in a *children's corner* in church or a crèche elsewhere, depending upon the message you want to give. Wherever it is, this should not be a black hole or the damp bit of the stage that nobody else will use, but a light, warm, cared-for place with carpets or rugs and appropriate furniture. It should be seen as a provision for those who want to use it rather than a ghetto for unwanted children.

  Similarly, the equipment should not resemble the left-overs from the jumble sale but should be cared for, in working order and clean. Appeals to the congregation for such items nearly always work, but you may wish to raise the profile of children's work in the church by submitting budget proposals to the PCC or inviting special contributions on an appropriate day such as the annual Thanksgiving for Baptism service.

These facilities should be available all the time but it is essential at a baptism service that newcomers and visitors are told where they are and that they can go to find them at any time during the service. Alternatively, they can be given to children as they arrive to take with them to the pews, or the preacher can invite children to go and get a picture to colour in during the sermon or the eucharistic prayer, which he or she will look forward to seeing at the end of the service (and will remember to do so). This incentive is important and, for all its simplicity and apparent insignificance, leads to a feeling of being valued.

It should be noted that the growth in Sunday trading is causing some churches to experiment with midweek and Saturday worship for the whole congregation, although this is not yet widespread practice.

Children receiving communion
– and confirmation

Traditionally, infant baptism has been seen as the natural forerunner to an adult decision made formally and publicly at confirmation. The two sacraments have gone hand in hand even though far more people are baptized than confirmed. For those families who remain or become committed to attendance at the Eucharist, issues arise regarding the participation of their children in worship. Children brought to church from birth may find themselves worshipping regularly for thirteen or fourteen years before they are allowed to share in the Communion service with their parents.

A more open and welcoming atmosphere within the Church and the revising of the meaning of baptismal vocation have led some dioceses to allow children to participate fully in the Eucharist before they come to confirmation. The argument runs that if baptism gives membership of the Church, then those who have been attending regularly and are part of the church family should be allowed to share fully in the benefits of communion at a younger age than before. The feeling of exclusion can lead to disenchantment, especially when the children may be more regular in attendance than many adults. Others argue that children are unable to understand the nature of the sacrament and what they are doing, but there are many confirmed adults of whom this could also be said. The question is whether rational and cognitive ability should dictate when and how a sacrament is received. Some would say that a parish operating an open baptism policy should be the first to consider open access to communion, but this is an issue which needs to be fully discussed with any congregation as it is an area of contention and needs careful handling.

If a parish chooses to pursue this, it does not mean that any and all children who present themselves at the altar rail will receive. A course of preparation and initiation into communion should be marked by a parish celebration as an important event rather than something that happens by default. The families and godparents should be invited to share in this important occasion and there should be some kind of formal welcome within the body of a full service, with declarations made by the children to be admitted and by the congregation who will support them, reminiscent of the baptismal vows. Your own diocese may have particular views and guidelines which should be consulted and the House of Bishops produced guidelines in March 1997 (GS Misc 488) which should be consulted before embarking on this.

The birth and rebirth of adult faith

The birth of a child is one of the most important events in the lives of parents and it is often at these times, in a rush of thanksgiving and depth of emotion, that they begin to question the deeper meaning of life and become aware of a sense of the spiritual. These are good times to build on this flickering flame and rekindle it. Baptism preparation will have started them thinking and their sense of acceptance and belonging will encourage them to enquire further.

It is the church's responsibility to cater for the whole family as well as the infant. Parents will learn with their children through family activities, but they need events and courses geared to adults only. They can be encouraged to join any of the current groups — the choir, the ringers, the men's breakfast group or whatever; they can be introduced to the house-group system; or they can be the founder members of a new group if a gap is identified.

Structured teaching courses are available and well publicized (Alpha or Emmaus, for example) and you may have ready-made courses to offer parents — which ones will depend on the style of your churchmanship and the approach you like to adopt. Parents also need some time and space, so take care that in your enthusiasm to rush them on to the next stage you do not overwhelm them.

Circumstances vary and those who are rarely free in the evenings because of business commitments may welcome guidance on private prayer and Bible study. Bible Reading Fellowship notes can be used on the train; others may discover a need to pray with others and be part of prayer circles.

All these things may lead some to a new declaration of faith through the act of confirmation and adult classes will provide the stimulus and teaching they require.

An easy mistake to make is to approach adults as potential recipients of what the church, the provider, has to offer, with scant thought for what the adults need. In this approach, the church is seen as a fixed institution which has all the answers and new adults as pegs to be fixed into ready-made holes.

Another thing which clergy can do to enable people to make the transition from enquirer to full member is to start where the adults are rather than where they think or hope they might be. This can be done in many ways, including:

- utilizing their skills and interests by inviting them to take an active role in the church in an area in which they have expertise, e.g. being invited to join the readers' or intercessors' rota so that they begin to own the church as theirs;

- finding out what questions *they* want to ask and what *they* want to learn about.

In one such group, called 'Making Connections', where the participants were invited to set the agenda, the kinds of questions posed included: 'What happens to the money we put in that dish?' 'Can I join the choir even though I'm divorced?' 'Who is the Lamb of God?' 'What's the difference between green and purple weeks?' 'What happens after the service in that little room where the vicar and curate go?' These questions led into all kinds of areas of study but meant that individuals felt they were being taken seriously and could move at their own pace.

Once again, it is easy for clergy to assume too much knowledge and underestimate the importance of such questions to enquirers. Even those with professional backgrounds and a good education may be totally ignorant of basic Christian matters; expertise and authority in one area of life do not mean that the same level of expertise is present in religious matters.

The baptism of infants, then, must be seen as an opportunity for reaching the parents and educating them in a way which will enthuse them and deepen their own commitment to Christ and his Church.

It is quite clear from the liturgy and the continuing interest in the education of congregations that baptism is most definitely one stage in the process of involvement in lifelong Christian discipleship. Thus the whole programme of worship, activities and teaching which a local church provides must be related in a holistic way, so that what happens at the rites of passage is linked into the whole orchestration of parish life. There may be high spots, and baptism will be one, but it should be part of the symphony rather than the solo instrument.

CONCLUSION

We have seen that the concept and practice of baptism has been a vital parts of the Christian heritage in Scripture and tradition. We have seen that reason and experience have contributed to the development of the liturgy from earliest times, culminating in the birth of a new liturgy for a new millennium.

We have found that, despite a wide variety of ideas, theology, policy and practice, it is quite clear that baptism matters to all Christians (and to many people on the edge of the Church and the edge of faith), but especially to those in leadership roles within the Church. This is why this book was commissioned and why we hope that you and your congregation will continue to give all the initiation rites a high priority in your theological reflection and ministerial practice.

The baptismal vocation, by which individuals become part of the body of Christ and the worldwide Christian Church, is the same today as it was yesterday; the content of a baptism service today would not be completely foreign to the early Church – and yet there are important contextual differences. Whether the enquirer is somebody who comes into church on a Monday morning on the off-chance that they will find the vicar there, or a fully-fledged member of the congregation conversant with the deepest meaning of Romans 6, *Common Worship* provides enough flexibility and permutations to suit all contexts and circumstances. It invites us all to revisit our experience and understanding of the liturgy both in theory and practice.

The crux of the matter is still the word 'commitment' and in his book *The New Archbishop Speaks*, George Carey expresses this well in his short chapter on baptism. 'When a new Christian in New Testament times went down into the waters of baptism, what was at stake was total commitment. This commitment was being displayed in three different ways, and it presents a challenge to us today.'[1] He goes on to describe God's commitment to his creation through his gracious and generous gifts, our commitment (albeit weak and incomplete) to God, and the commitment of the congregation (representative of the whole Church) to all those who come seeking baptism.

The outworking of these commitments is what much of Christian faith and ministry is about. This is the ministry to which we are still called and to which we respond. *Common Worship* enables us to do that in ways which assure us that whatever else may be going out of fashion, baptism still matters.

APPENDIX

CANON LAW

Priests of the Church of England are legally and morally bound to observe Canon Law in the area of baptismal policy as in all others. All those involved in conducting baptisms should be familiar with the contents of sections B21–26 which are reproduced in full here and referred to in appropriate chapters.

B21 OF HOLY BAPTISM

It is desirable that every minister having a cure of souls shall normally administer the sacrament of Holy Baptism on Sundays at public worship when the most number of people come together, that the congregation there present may witness the receiving of them that be newly baptised into Christ's Church, and be put in remembrance of their own profession made to God in their baptism.

B22 OF THE BAPTISM OF INFANTS

1. Due notice, normally of at least a week, shall be given before a child is brought to the church to be baptised.

2. If the minister shall refuse or unduly delay to baptise any such infant, the parents or guardians may apply to the bishop of the diocese, who shall, after consultation with the minister, give such directions as he thinks fit.

3. The minister shall instruct the parents or guardians of an infant to be admitted to Holy Baptism that the same responsibilities rest on them as are in the service of Holy Baptism required of the godparents.

4. No minister shall refuse or, save for the purpose of preparing or instructing the parents or guardians or godparents, delay to baptise any infant within his cure that is brought to the church to be baptised, provided that due notice has been given and the provisions relating to godparents in these Canons are observed.

5.   A minister who intends to baptise any infant whose parents are residing outside the boundaries of his cure, unless the names of such persons or of one of them be on the church electoral roll of the same, shall not proceed to the baptism without having sought the good will of the minister of the parish in which such parents reside.

6.   No minister being informed of the weakness or danger of death of any infant within his cure and therefore desired to go to baptise the same shall either refuse or delay to do so.

7.   A minister so baptising a child in a hospital or nursing home, the parents of the child not being resident in his cure, nor their names on the church electoral roll of the same, shall send their names and address to the minister of the parish in which they reside.

8.   If any infant which is privately baptised do afterwards live, it shall be brought to the church and there, by the minister, received into the congregation of Christ's flock according to the form and manner prescribed in and by the office for Private Baptism authorised by Canon B1.

9.   The minister of every parish shall warn the people that without grave cause and necessity they should not have their children baptised privately in their houses.

B23 OF GODPARENTS AND SPONSORS

1.   For every child to be baptised there shall be not fewer than three godparents, of whom at least two shall be of the same sex as the child and of whom at least one shall be of the opposite sex; save that, when three cannot conveniently be had, one god-father and godmother shall suffice. Parents may be godparents for their own children provided that the child have at least one other godparent.

2.   The godparents shall be persons who will faithfully fulfil their responsibilities both by their care for the children committed to their charge and by the example of their own godly living.

3.   When one who is of riper years is to be baptised he shall choose three, or at least two, to be his sponsors, who shall be ready to present him at the font and afterwards put him in mind of his Christian profession and duties.

4. No person shall be admitted to be a sponsor or godparent who has not been baptised and confirmed. Nevertheless the minister shall have power to dispense with the requirement of confirmation in any case in which in his judgement need so requires.

B24 OF THE BAPTISM OF SUCH AS ARE OF RIPER YEARS

1. When any such person as is of riper years and able to answer for himself is to be baptised, the minister shall instruct such person, or cause him to be instructed, in the principles of the Christian religion, and exhort him so to prepare himself with prayers and fasting that he may receive this holy sacrament with repentance and faith.

2. At least a week before any such baptism is to take place, the minister shall give notice thereof to the bishop of the diocese or whomsoever he shall appoint for the purpose.

3. Every person thus baptised shall be confirmed by the bishop so soon after his baptism as conveniently may be; that so he may be admitted to the Holy Communion.

B25 OF THE SIGN OF THE CROSS IN BAPTISM

The Church of England has ever held and taught, and holds and teaches still, that the sign of the Cross used in baptism is no part of the substance of the sacrament: but, for the remembrance of the Cross, which is very precious to those that rightly believe in Jesus Christ, has retained the sign of it in baptism, following therein the primitive and apostolic Churches.

B26 OF TEACHING THE YOUNG

1. Every minister shall take care that the children and young people within his cure are instructed in the doctrine, sacraments and discipline of Christ, as the Lord has commanded and as they are set forth in the holy Scriptures, in the Book of Common Prayer, and especially in the Church Catechism; and to this end he, or some godly and competent persons appointed by him, shall on Sundays or if need be at other convenient times diligently instruct and teach them in the same.

2. All parents and guardians shall take care that their children receive such instruction.

NOTES

CHAPTER 1: THE SACRAMENT OF BAPTISM

1   Alister McGrath, *Christian Theology, an Introduction*, Blackwells, 1994, p. 428.
2   Article XXV of the Articles of Religion.
3   Alister McGrath, *Christian Theology*, p. 434.
4   Article XXV of the Articles of Religion.
5   Genesis 12 and 15.
6   Exodus 24.
7   Matthew 3.13-17; Mark 1.9-11; Luke 3.21-22.
8   John 1. 29-34.
9   Morna Hooker, *The Gospel According to St Mark*, A. & C. Black, 1993.
10 Mark 16.15-16.
11 Matthew 28.19-20.
12 Luke 24.47.
13 John 3.23.
14 Acts 2. 37-42.
15 Acts 16.33.
16 Acts 8.36-39.
17 Acts 8.9-13.
18 Acts 16.14-15.
19 Acts 10.44-48.
20 Acts 10.44-48; 11.15-18.
21 Acts 19.1-7.
22 Acts 8.36-39.
23 Acts 16.14-15.
24 Acts 2.37-42.
25 Acts 9.17-19.
26 Romans 6.3.
27 1 Corinthians 6.11.
28 1 Corinthians 12.13.
29 Romans 6.3-8.
30 Romans 6.1-4.
31 Ephesians 4.4-6.
32 Galations 3.27

CHAPTER 2: ANGLICAN BAPTISMAL POLICY

[1] Canon B22.

[2] Acts 2.41.

[3] Anonymous communication.

[4] Revd Nigel Nicholson, incumbent, Cranleigh Parish Church.

[5] John Macquarrie, *A Guide to the Sacraments*, SCM Press, 1997, p. 6.

CHAPTER 4: BAPTISM PREPARATION

[1] *Baptism* leaflet, National Society/Church House Publishing, 1998.

[2] Revd Christopher Blissard-Barnes, incumbent, Newdigate Parish Church.

[3] Revd Dr Andrew Norman, incumbent, St Nicolas Parish Church, Guildford.

CHAPTER 5: GODPARENTS

[1] *Common Worship: Initiation Services*, 1998: Questions to Parents and Godparents.

[2] *Becoming a Godparent* leaflet, National Society/Church House Publishing, 1998.

[3] *Common Worship: Initiation Services*, 1998.

CHAPTER 6: THE BAPTISM SERVICE: USING THE NEW LITURGY

[1] See *On the Way*, Church House Publishing, 1995.

[2] Betty Pedley and John Muir, *Children in the Church?*, National Society/Church House Publishing, 1997.

[3] 1 Samuel 10.1.

[4] Luke 7.38.

[5] Acts 2.38.

[6] Revelation 3.4.

[7] All the prayers in this section are by the authors unless otherwise stated.

[8] Christopher Herbert, *Prayers for Children*, National Society/Church House Publishing, 1993, p. 105.

[9] St Anselm, 1033–1109.

[10] Attributed to St Benedict, 480–543.

CHAPTER 7: TALKS AND RESOURCES FOR BAPTISM SERVICES

[1] Richard Giles, *Repitching the Tent*, Canterbury Press, 1977.

CHAPTER 8: AFTER BAPTISM — WHAT NEXT?

[1] Hilary Brabon.
[2] Jill Barnett.
[3] John Westerhoff, *Will Our Children Have Faith?* Harper & Row, 1976.

CONCLUSION

[1] George Carey, *The New Archbishop Speaks*, Lion Publishing, 1991.

BIBLIOGRAPHY AND RESOURCES

Baptism leaflet, National Society/Church House Publishing, 1998

Becoming a Godparent leaflet, National Society/Church House Publishing, 1998

Colin Buchanan, a variety of Grove Booklets relating to baptism, available from Grove Books, Ridley Hall Road, Cambridge CB3 9HU

George Carey, *The New Archbishop Speaks*, Lion Publishing, 1991

Common Worship: Initiation Services, Church House Publishing, 1998

John Finney, *Finding Faith Today*, British and Foreign Bible Society, 1992

Richard Giles, *Repitching the Tent*, Canterbury Press, 1997

Michael Green, *Baptism: Its Purpose, Practice and Power*, Hodder & Stoughton, 1987

Christopher Herbert, *Prayers for Children*, National Society/Church House Publishing, 1993

Joachim Jeremias, *Infant Baptism in the First Four Centuries*, SCM Press, 1960

Mark and Helen Johnson, *Songs for Every Christmas; Songs for Every Day; Songs for Every Easter; Songs for Every Season,* Out of the Ark Music, School House, Esher Green, Esher, Surrey [music, words, cassette and CD available]

Jump Up if You're Wearing Red, National Society/Church House Publishing, 1996

Graham Kendrick, *The Source,* Kevin Mayhew, 1998 (songs)

W. G. Kümmel, *The Theology of the New Testament*, SCM Press, 1972

Gordon Kuhrt, *Believing in Baptism*, Mowbray, 1987

John Macquarrie, *A Guide to the Sacraments*, SCM Press, 1997

Phil Moon and Jonathan Roberts, *Making Confirmation Count*, Church House Publishing, 1994

On the Way: Towards an Integrated Approach to Christian Initiation, The General Synod of the Church of England, Church House Publishing, 1995

Betty Pedley and John Muir, *Children in the Church?*, National Society/Church House Publishing, 1997 (all-age baptism worship)

Oliver Quick, *The Christian Sacraments*, Fontana, 1964

Gavin Reid, *To Be Confirmed*, Hodder & Stoughton, 1994

Martin Robinson, *The Faith of the Unbeliever*, CPAS, 1994

Kenneth Stevenson, *The Mystery of Baptism in the Anglican Tradition*, Canterbury Press, 1998

Sharon Swain, *Calling You*, Mowbray, 1993

Sharon Swain, *Exploring Confirmation*, Mothers' Union, 1994

This Is Our Faith (Anglican version), Redemptorist Press, 1996

Stuart Thomas, *Confirmation to Follow*, Kevin Mayhew, 1996

Stuart Thomas, *Come to the Feast*, Kevin Mayhew, 1997 (talks)

A Dictionary of Christian Theology, ed. A. Richardson, SCM Press, 1969

The Illustrated Bible Dictionary, Inter-Varsity Press, 1997

The Oxford Dictionary of the Christian Church, ed. F. L. Cross and E. A. Livingstone, Oxford University Press, 1993

Geoffrey W. Bromiley, *Theological Dictionary of the New Testament*, Eerdmans, 1985

INDEX

Index